The Jedi Academy Online Presents:
Exploring the Jedi Lifestyle

The Jedi Academy Online Presents:
Exploring the Jedi Lifestyle

K.S. Trout
The Jedi Academy Online

jediacademyonline.com
Valencia, California

Publisher: CreateSpace.com
The Jedi Academy Online
Valencia CA. 91354
USA
Telephone Number: (On Request)
Web Site: http://jediacademyonline.com
E-Mail: admin@jediacademyonline.com
Copyright © 2013 The Jedi Academy Online

All Rights Reserved. No part of this publication may be reproduced, stored in a retrieval system or transmitted in any form by any means without prior permission of the copyright owner.
Inquires Should be Made to the Jedi Academy Online.

Every effort has been made to ensure that this book is free from error or omissions. However, the Publisher, the Author, the Editor or their respective employees or agents, shall not accept responsibility for injury, loss or damage occasioned to any person acting or refraining from action as a result of material in this book whether or not such injury, loss or damage is in any way due to any negligent act or omission, breach of duty or default on the part of the Publisher, the Author, the Editor or their respective employees or agents.

Acknowledgments, References, and Disclaimers:
George Lucas, Lucasfilms LTD., and Disney - All Star Wars related material Copyright and Trademark of Lucasfilms LTD. and Disney All Rights Reserved.
Power of the Jedi Sourcebook – Copyright 2002 Lucasfilms LTD. All Rights Reserved.
Star Wars Roleplaying Guide 2nd Edition – Copyright 1996 Lucasfilms LTD. All Rights Reserved.
Jedi Apprentice Series - Jude Watson. Copyright Lucasfilms LTD. All Rights Reserved.
Jedi Academy Online – Copyright 2007-2013 Outlaw Kings Productions
I'd like to give Special Thanks to: Carolyn and Dennis Blundell, Jaden Palmer, the entire JAO membership, and to Shelley Jane Reece.

Author: K.S. Trout
Title: The Jedi Academy Online Presents: Exploring the Jedi Lifestyle.
ISBN-13: 978-1482339710
ISBN-10: 1482339714

Editor:
Cover Design: Opie Macleod © 2013
Page Design: Opie Macleod © 2013
Printed and Bound: CreateSpace and Amazon.com

<u>This Book is Dedicated to my families.</u> My parents, my Jedi family, and my sanity-savior Pace. Without each of you none of this would be possible.

Contents

Chapter 1: Our First Steps into a Larger World
Introduction.. 1
How to Use This Book...................................... 5
Personal Note.. 7

Chapter 2: Our Foundation
Introduction.. 9
Jedi Code... 10
Jedi Circle.. 11
Five Goals of the Jedi................. 12
Jedi Rules of Behavior... 13

Chapter 3: Tier One Training Program
Introduction Lesson... 15
Lesson One.. 41
Lesson Two... 72
Lesson Three............................... 96
Lesson Four................... 122
Lesson Five........ 150

Chapter 4: Supplemental Lessons
The Jedi Method.. 171
Exploring the Force... 177
The Dark Side... 179
Jediism – The Jedi Religion....... 183

Chapter 5: Conclusion
Resources... 188

Our First Steps Into a Larger World

Introduction:

Believe it or not there are many people who have been so inspired by the Jedi in Star Wars that they have sought to live their lives in a similar manner. To follow and adhere to the same ethics and moral codes as the Jedi as presented through Star Wars media. There are also others who are seeking a path of self-betterment. They wish to improve themselves, to become the people they want to be and know they can be. After reading over the concepts of the Jedi lifestyle many chose this road to that goal. Obviously there are many paths out there in the world, many roads to take. This is simply a brief exploration of one of the roads which just happens to share a rather known media label.

In 1977 George Lucas introduced Star Wars into the movie theaters and a franchise was born. To this day the Star Wars franchise is still going strong releasing new blockbuster content in various forms. This space saga sparked the imagination of millions and has inspired many in a variety of ways. One of those inspirations deals in philosophy, in lifestyle, in how one lives and interacts with the world. This may seem impossible or simply crazy to have a science-fiction franchise inspire philosophy and produce life-affirming material, but that is exactly what the Jedi Knights of Star Wars have done.

The Jedi. George Lucas took inspiration from many places and created an order and concept to be the guiding element of his hero within Star Wars. The Jedi and the Force were core aspects which helped turned Luke Skywalker from borcd farmboy to galactic hero. It was this order and this concept of the Force that caught the imagine of thousands, if not millions, of people. And it started the wheels on something George Lucas had hoped it would, spiritual questioning. Looking deeper into the spirit, into the self, and asking core and important questions on life and what else may exist out there.

In 1997 the Star Wars saga was re-released into the

theaters re-igniting the imagines of fans and introducing Star Wars to a new generation. However the ease and access of the computers and more importantly the internet started something new. The ease of communication allowed fans to connect to ways they were never able to before. This caused ideas and new forms entertainment to grow. From 1997 to 1999 an online fan-base was growing and creating new ways to experience Star Wars; online role-playing. Create a character in the Star Wars universe and share the journey and saga along with others. The homo-erectus of Star Wars gaming compared to the evolved platform of Star Wars: The Old Republic which currently exists.

    A few people from this group found through experience that many of the ideals and lessons created for their Jedi character could be applied to real-life with beneficial outcomes. They acknowledged the benefits of actively practicing patience, working on communication skills, of working on peace within. It was here others noted the similarities to existing ideas and paths out there. It was concepts like these that started a new thought - can one be a real life Jedi? Many began to explore the validity of the Jedi Philosophy found within Star Wars to determine the answer. As more people began this exploration the results were encouraging. Jedi Philosophy had something to it. It was proving itself to be a beneficial way of life which resolved a lot of life problems for those who followed it seriously. But how, why? How is it that science-fiction can actually offer advice beneficial to everyday life?

    These questions spurred people into new questions. They found interesting ideas, concepts, and so explored the various questions and practices which were put forth by the fictional Jedi. Is there a Universal Force that guides all things? Is calm and being at peace a true way to tap into this world? Is fear and aggression truly something dark? Can one truly be objective? Can we truly be at peace in this chaotic world?

    The interest in these types of questions hasn't vanished for thousands of years. We continue to find new ways to explore these age-old questions. The Jedi Philosophy is simply one more path in the world seeking to make some sense of the world we live in. The Jedi Path is built upon an idea that we need to be in the right place in our lives to be able to fully explore and understanding these deep questions of spirituality. Thus self-improvement is a major focus on the Jedi Path. We seek Physical, Mental, Emotional, Spiritual, Environmental, and Social Well-Being. It is this overall focus on World-Betterment through Self-Betterment. An idea that we affect the world around us just by living and that we should shoulder the responsibility of affecting our world in a positive manner.

This has been called the information age due to the ease of access to various knowledge, practices, and ideals out there. With the internet many ideas have found a worldwide audience in which to share, explore, and grow. A lot of these neoteric ideas, pseudo-philosophies, and new age religions would not have survived to the degree they do now if it weren't for the ease of communication we currently have. We can see the influence spread worldwide with Western Culture being flooded with Eastern philosophies, religions, and practices. Likewise we can see Western Culture having an influence all over the world from political ideals to social practices. This has encouraged an age of spiritual exploration within the world as well.

The goal of this book is to talk about and share the core of Jedi Philosophy. We will explore its basic foundations, seeking to give a general understanding of this new philosophical group. As well as shows the difference between Jediism, the religious movement, and the standard Jedi Philosophy prevalent today. Any way you look at it Jedi Philosophy is a new and very young concept. We will be looking to establish the core ideals accepted throughout the Jedi Community.

There have been a couple of attempts to write about this philosophy and lifestyle. Unfortunately none of those books have established anything creditable. They have lacked in objectivity, in clear explanation, and sought to fulfill a personal agenda. In fact one of the more known books is by Matthew Vossler. Unfortunately Vossler has never been a part of the Jedi

Community nor took the time to truly understand the history, development, and practices of the Jedi Philosophy. This has been a problem with most publications and media attention in regards to the Jedi.

There is a need to give a clear and objective voice to a budding ideology. To allow it to be told in a fair manner from one who has seen all sides and angles of the subject. Obviously talking about a philosophy taken from a fictional source raises many questions, especially in the realm of validity. Can a philosophy based upon a fictional source prove viable? Does Jedi Philosophy actually have merit or is it truly regurgitated new age non-sense which does not deserve the time of day? One can laugh at the terminology, the source of the ideas, but if they inspire personal betterment or growth? If they inspire one to explore their spiritual, mental, and physical well-being? If it inspires one to be a better person? Then does it truly matter the source, the name? What matters more, practical application or a practical name?

So we will be giving a brief look into the various ideals of the Jedi Philosophy. Each topic could be explored more in-depth. We could look into comparable philosophies, we could measure the validity by weighing what is out there now versus what the Jedi offer currently. We could discuss and explore ideas like the five goals of the Jedi in a much more in-depth manner. Yet this is an introduction, a way to offer insight into the Jedi Philosophy without drowning the reader in a information overload. A chance to form an opinion on the core ideals themselves rather than the in-depth reasoning behind them. A beginner's look at the philosophy to decide if it is worth further exploration.

How Jedi go about living this concept is the foundation being presented here. Exploring the philosophical core of the Jedi Path is something I find to be a worthwhile endeavor. Hopefully you will enjoy the journey as much as I have.

How to Approach this Book:

This book will be providing the Tier One Training Program that the Jedi Academy Online website uses. It was felt that this method provided the best approach to show how Jedi live and how they approach life and their own personal well-being. The program however is set-up for an online interactive format. It is important to note this as I am going to be leaving in the homework assignments for that type of format. It is my hope that this encourages you to start your own training journal. A notebook to keep your thoughts, reflections, progress, opinions, assignments, and your own ideas on how to better incorporate the ideas presented within the Jedi ideology.

This program is an introductory system. It is not meant to be extremely in-depth. It is not meant to provide all answers. As mentioned, it is meant for an interactive environment which allows for questions and concerns to be asked and addressed openly and freely. If you are not a member at the jediacademyonline.com website, I recommend joining. Outside of that, please remember that this is the first steps. This is not a 10 steps to being a Jedi Master. Going through this book provides you with experience, understanding, information, knowledge, but not titles, privileges, or magic powers. This isn't a five keys to a successful life. This is simply what Jedi do, what they live, what they follow, believe, incorporate into their daily lives. This is what you can expect from any Jedi you may meet. Chances are greater than you think. There are thousands of Jedi world-wide. The beauty of the internet and self-discipline – means ideas can be transmitted without boarders and barriers.

Important: There are physical exercises listed within the program. First, be smart, double-check with your doctor. If you have a shoulder injury than do Not "power-through" push-ups. Seek an alternative. Talk with your physician about comparable exercises. We are not responsible for your silliness. So please, be responsible – it is one of the cornerstones of the Jedi lifestyle. Responsibility, Integrity, Accountability, so do the proper thing. Get cleared before making major changes to your diet and exercises routine. We are encouraging a healthy lifestyle. Simple fitness daily with good eating habits to promote physical health which does a play a part on mental and emotional health. So take it serious and seek out professional in-person advice.

Lastly I want to mention that this is the offline hard copy for students already in the Tier One Training Program. This is their textbook if you will. It goes hand-and-hand with interaction, discussion, and access to veteran Jedi such as myself. If you take part in this book and want to pursue the Jedi Path further you are welcome to join us at our website. However this book does not grandfather you ahead. You will be expected to repeat the program at the website. This is done for a couple of reasons.

First is simply having that oversight. It makes a difference to have someone looking over your work. Making the subtle adjustments that might be necessary. One can learn a lot on their own, but there is a great benefit to have confirmation from someone who has been there. To get years of experience saying, yes good work or providing that correction.

Second is accountability. Every individual who wears the Jedi name at the Jedi Academy Online has not only the JAO stamp of approval, but my personal endorsement as well. In this I have to be as sure as possible that one who says, "I am a Jedi at the Jedi Academy Online." Will in fact represent our site, our ideals, our path in a positive way. That they will and are in fact living the Jedi Way. Online interaction helps in this, especially with modern media. Skype video calls, phone conversations, text messages, real-time chats, connected through facebook. All of these tools allow us to get a better understanding of our fellow Jedi. We also meet in-person, individually, as a group. In this I am comfortable with giving the thumbs up to any Jedi at the JAO. And it is exactly why I will not endorse any other Jedi site. I simply cannot vouch for them. This is why completing this book on your own grants no titles at the JAO website.

Personal Note:

The Jedi Academy Online is (at this time) not affiliated with LucasFilms, Disney, or any companies or subsidiaries related to those corporations. This is strictly a personal exploration of an educational topic which I have spent the majority of my life studying and working on.

I label the Jedi as a neoteric philosophy which I feel will only grow in time. Perhaps even eventually out-growing the fiction which inspired the idea. The Jedi philosophy is an idea which has inspired people to explore the world, the mysteries of the world (both spiritual and more tangible), and their own self-betterment. I see it and have experienced it as a positive and beneficial way of life.

For the past 15 years I have been a part of an online community which has explored the validity of actually and truly applying Jedi philosophy to everyday life. I have grown with the Jedi as the core focus of my life. I majored in philosophy at college because of the Jedi. I graduated a police academy because of the Jedi. I became a bartender because it became clear Jedi is a lifestyle not a career. It is okay to laugh, I am. When younger I didn't realize the difference between how you live and what you do. I didn't get the importance of financial well-being, of financial independence until much later in life. Ironically enough it was the Jedi concepts which drilled it into my head. Being a Jedi doesn't pay – financially. But it does pay big in peace of mind, spirit, and body. I may not be rich, but I am certainly happy and fulfilled. Now I can work on that rich part, but it won't be fulfilled via the Jedi. I feel this is important disclaimer. Just as much as trying to save my bacon from Disney lawyers.

Be a Jedi because you see benefit in it. Because you believe and experience it as a positive way to live your life. Which provides useful and applicable concepts which are beneficial in your everyday life. No delusions of grandeur allowed – Deal?

Our Foundation

Introduction:

I want to provide you with basic core texts Jedi use and refer to on a daily basis. All without any explanation or added thoughts. This is simply the texts themselves. I feel offering this allows you to consider your own thought son how these apply to your life. As well as give some food for thought as some you may not agree with until you understand what we mean by them.

All of these texts will be explored much more in-depth in this book. These texts can have a book to them alone in my opinion. Really each individual concept could have its own book. Some you see this already. Topics like meditation and physical fitness have thousands of books on them. It can seem overwhelming to apply all these elements to your life.

Remember that is the point of the tier training system. To help people slowly, but surely apply the ideals to their life and see positive results. Nothing is overnight. It does take time, so have patience with yourself and the material. If you find a concept you'd like it explore further I encourage it. Unfortunately, at this point in time, I will not be able to provide the depth of information on the topics as I would like.

Some people seek to memorize these elements. To use them as mantras or simply help focus their mind on embodying a specific trait. That can be difficult to do when it broken down in a lecture format. When you are reading and taking in other information related to the texts. So I really just wanted to give a clean and clear – untouched look at these pillars of Jedi Thought. Hopefully it helps and provides useful.

The Jedi Code:

The Jedi Code has gone through several changes over years through the various fiction writers of Star Wars. Some are more applicable than others. Some serve better as a mantra. At the Jedi Academy Online we use call is often called the five line version of the Jedi Code. So this is the version we will sharing. Remember that we will be exploring the history and variations of the Jedi Code later on.

For now I simply want to share the Jedi Code as is. Allow you to puzzle over one of the core and oldest guiding principles the Jedi have had. When I first started in the Jedi community, this was the guiding star. This is what you had to master to progress. It still holds as a staple of Jedi thought. This is one of common denominators you'll find across all Jedi. From Jediism, to Jedi Realism, to the Jedi Academy Online, we all teach and pass on the Jedi Code.

There is no emotion; there is peace.

-=-

There is no ignorance; there is knowledge.

-=-

There is no passion; there is serenity.

-=-

There is no chaos; there is harmony.

-=-

There is no death; there is the Force.

The Jedi Circle:

The Jedi Circle, unlike the Jedi Code, did not come from Star Wars. Rather it was created by myself based upon my experience and studies of living as a Jedi. I use to have a little saying before the Jedi Circle. It went, *"The Jedi walks the circle. They live the five practices, which enforce the five tenets, which nurture the five traits, which bring the five truths, which counteract the five misconceptions."*

The Jedi Circle has two versions as well. One version removes the five misconceptions and uses the five goals of the Jedi. Here this book, I'll be looking at the five goals separately, so that is why we are using this version of the Jedi Circle.

The Five Practices: Meditation, Diplomacy, Awareness, Physical Fitness, and Self-Discipline.

-=-

The Five Tenets: Peace, Knowledge, Serenity, Harmony, the Force.

-=-

The Five Traits: Patience, Objectivity, Reliability, Humility, Wisdom.

-=-

The Five Truths: Self-Honesty, Learning, Guidance, Sacrifice, Commitment.

-=-

The Five Misconceptions: Star Wars, Religion, Segregation, Compassion, Infallible.

The Five Goals of the Jedi:

The Five Goals of the Jedi are meant to replace the five misconceptions when the Jedi have overcome those misunderstandings. However, just because the Jedi as a whole still deal with those issues does not mean the Jedi are without purpose or direction. That we just forget why we do what we do.

There is the inherent lifestyle we chose to live. A we each have our own personal reasons for following the Jedi Way. All Jedi support and seek self-improvement as well as like the idea of world-betterment through self-betterment. Each person doing their duty to ensure a richer environment to experience. Despite this we do have core goals which all Jedi embrace. They are as follows.

Train Diligently

-=-

Render Aid

-=-

Provide Support

-=-

Defend Those in Need

-=-

Study the Force

The Jedi Rules of Behavior:

This is another list born from the fiction. Or more accurately, from the role-playing guides. These supplement the other concepts pretty well and simply added a little more understanding. Some of the five goals were taken from this text. So you will notice some overlap. Of course that should be a recurring theme. Some subjects and ideas are simply approached in a variety of ways because they are multifaceted concepts. Like the rest we will discuss this more later on in the book.

1 Self-Discipline.
2 Conquer Arrogance.
3 Conquer Overconfidence.
4 Conquer Defeatism.
5 Conquer Stubbornness.
-=-
6 Conquer Recklessness.
7 Conquer Curiosity.
8 Conquer Aggression.
9 Conquer External Loyalties.
10 Conquer Materialism.
-=-
11 Responsibility.
12 Practice Honesty.
13 Honor Your Promises.
14 Honor the Jedi Order.
15 Honor the Law.
-=-
16 Honor Life.
17 Public Service.
18 Render Aid.
19 Defend the Weak.
20 Provide Support.

Tier One Training Program

Introduction:

From this point forward I am going to share the information most identically as it is presented on our website. In this some of the verbiage may seem a bit off. I apologize for that. I have sought to approach this with a book format, however I really want to encourage online participation. The best to do that without constantly writing out - go to the jediacademyonline.com/forum/index.php for further feedback – is to simply approach this in the same manner as the website.

In a previous book I provided lined pages for assignments. That would just take up a lot of pages. I am not entirely sure how useful that really is, so I have foregone adding those in this book. If I get requests I may make a revision. In which case all this space will be explaining about that. Nice filler right? Okay, I am going to get serious here. Lets begin Tier One Jedi Training.

First I want welcome all reading this and thank you for your time and consideration. If you are new to the concept of Jedi Philosophy I am sure this all seems a bit strange to you, but hopefully we can alleviate any concerns and answer any questions you may have. If you are not new to the idea, then I hope you enjoy exploring a different approach to the Jedi Path and training.

The Jedi Academy Online Training Program is broken into Tiers or Levels. There are currently a total of Four Complete Training Tiers one can go through. Each offering its own structure, time-frame, and unique lessons. Tier One is straight forward with One Main Lesson per Week for Six Weeks - with supplemental lessons offered throughout each week. If you stick to the order and layout, it shouldn't be as confusing as it sounds.

You won't find any titles here at the Jedi Academy Online outside of denoting one's experience Level within our program. This is because we focus on living as Jedi in our everyday lives and if we are doing that all else is transitory. We denote experience progression simply as a way for visitors and new members know who has gone through what. This way if you have a question about Tier Three you are not asking someone who has not gone through that process yet; in other words it is purely organizational.

Jedi Philosophy or real Jedi training if you will, is focused on physical, mental, emotional, social, and spiritual well-being and improvement. Our focus is bettering the self so that we may better the world around us. There is a shift in focus, in the beginning we focus on the ourselves, where we are at, our development, and learning to live and apply the Jedi ideals to our everyday lives. From there our awareness grows to others and our focus becomes much more about other people. How our actions affect the world and people around us.

If you are looking for cool Force Powers like moving objects with your mind or have images of flashy lightsabers in your head, I am sorry to disappoint, but that will not be found here. Our approach at the JAO is very grounded and has a very practical focus to the Jedi Path. You will not find physic powers, astral plane, or magic taught here. Likewise we look at the spiritual as a very personal thing, so while we explore spiritual concepts no religion, belief, or deity will be pushed upon anyone here. We do not, as an organization, label or teach that the Jedi Path is a religion and keep an open mind to all religious and cultural beliefs of individual Jedi. What you will get here is basic academic study - research, application, lectures, homework. It can be a bit boring for some - we focus on diplomacy, patience, and we trust those here to live the lessons (else why be here). And while we do have our fun and laughs, we do have fun offline get-togethers you can join, mostly it is an online learning experience. If that still works for you - glad to have you with us.

How to Start Tier One:

1.) Read the Introduction Lesson - this not only tells you what to expect, but also gives you a beginner's lesson to help you understand how the process works. It has core information and sets up how the Tier One process will work.

2.) Simply follow the Lessons in Order, paying close attention to the Due Dates (in later tiers the due dates may be switched on you - have to pay attention). Each Lesson is One Week long, but they have supplemental lessons you can do to stay involved and active. These supplemental lessons are only a day long.

3.) Be Sincere, and You will Succeed. Read, Apply, Live. These are meant to help one not only understand Jedi thought, but to live as a Jedi in their everyday lives. No Jedi Master to sit over your shoulder and make you do any of it. It falls on you to either complete or not. Your experience, your results depend solely on your involvement, on your commitment. If you coast through the lessons, simply read and reply, you aren't going to get much out of it.

4.) Do Not try to guess a "right" answer. Allow the practices, allow the exercises, and assignments guide you to Your OWN conclusion. Be Honest with yourself most of all, but be honest with us and we can be of help, we can offer the best thoughts on your progress. Don't play Jedi, be a Jedi. It really isn't as crazy as it sounds I promise.

Introduction Lesson:

First thing, this is an introduction lesson to help one see how the lesson structure is set-up and get use to how we do our training at this site. Also this allows me to introduce you to the atmosphere, mindset, and ideals of this group. In this you can decide whether or not to devote your time here or seek your Jedi learning elsewhere. The Jedi Community is a diverse place and some sites/groups will fit you better than others.

As the founder of the Jedi Academy Online (or JAO for short) I created this place originally for me. To better myself, to help me formulate, cement, and advance my training and ideals of the Jedi Path. This is the place I was looking when I began on the Jedi Path. No other Jedi Organization/Website/Group out there is, can be, or was what the Jedi Academy Online is. There was no place for me to succeed as a Jedi, to be a Jedi. All places I saw simply played Jedi online. No one was pushing people to BE Jedi. When a Jedi felt pain they were given a pass, they were allowed to be less than what they should be. It was okay for them to fail. When I was going through a hard time in my life, instead of enforcing the Jedi Ideals I was allowed to act like a spoiled child. That is not what you will find here.

"We all want. We all give to get what we want." - Mass Effect 2. We have all suffered, we will suffer, not because we want to, but because life is built on a give and take system. Nothing lasts forever and we never know when the things we love, the things we value, the things we worked hard for will disappear from our lives. Horrible things happen in life, everyday there are horrors happening in the world. Things happen in life which can knock us to the ground and we can feel the best option is to just give-in, to give-up, and surrender to the power of life. Until we leave this world, this will never change. We will be tested, we will be challenged, life will be there to offer another chance to fall. Yet there is always the flip-side, we each have the strength and ability to grow and progress through difficult times.

Is that not why we are here? Because we refuse to bow to the darkness of life. We seek the strength to stand when we want nothing more than to lay down. We see the beauty, we see the elegance, we see the power in life; in light, in darkness, we see the beauty of struggle and growth. We see the value in life. What we are looking for is not some love and light in this world, because we can already see it. What we are looking for is a way to empower ourselves, to grab that beauty and turn it into something just as powerful within us. To be a Force, to be a Light, to be a Jedi within a world that needs such people. To stand up strong even when we would rather lay down.

It is not an easy thing to be a Jedi. For so many reasons it is not easy to be a Jedi. It is a process and you cannot wake-up tomorrow and simply be a Jedi. No one was born a Jedi, it takes dedication, it takes commitment, it takes waking up every single morning and being a Jedi. Let me tell you what the JAO expects from you - every single day:

We demand you give 70 minutes of your day for physical fitness. We demand that you give 30 minutes a day for meditation. We demand that you give at the very least 5 hours a week to study (breakdown of these times is found later on and doesn't count other time requests such as community service). If you can't find the time then you have to look in at what matters most to you.

What is more important to you? Who do you want to be? If you just want to be a Gamer, than be that, embrace it. Video games have a lot of great philosophical concepts to consider and while that fluctuates exploring such tough topics is on the rise in that field. But if you tell me you can't find the time, that you are too busy, then you will find a problem awaiting you here. I say here, because we can point you to much more relaxed places. Much more inviting, much more part-time sites which will gently encourage your individual growth. Sure we understand that life gets busy, that we must make cuts in our time, but if video games and television get priority over Jedi practices and living then that is an issue.

Know now that a Jedi has to make sacrifices at times. The

first challenge you are going to face is what you are willing to sacrifice to become something more. No one becomes a Jedi by sitting and playing games. No one becomes a Jedi by make-believe. It requires time, it requires action, it requires you to be what you have chosen to be. There are no excuses, there is life and what you do with it. Everyone has the power of choice, everyone is free to make choices in their life. The question you face right now is do I truly want to be a Jedi? A Jedi - consider that for a moment.

Truly, are you prepared for this? Is this what you want? Are you ready for someone to be poking at your life, your choices, and demanding, absolutely demanding the very best every single day from you? Are you truly looking to become an actual Jedi? I tell you now - I am not always nice, I have a different take on the Jedi Lifestyle, I believe in emotional content, I believe in passionate words, I believe in not only confronting our pain but embracing it. I will push for the best and when you act like a jackmonkey I will call you a jackmonkey. Much nicer places to train than here, but I promise you one thing, if you want to find your absolute best, you'll find it here.

Here is the thing. I want Jedi I can trust. You say you are a Jedi, then I will give you the keys to my house, babysit, borrow my car. When someone here says they did something that is all the proof I need. Jedi = Integrity. Responsibility. Dedication. I'll tell my darkest secrets to a Jedi to seek their advice, that is what I expect and demand. I demand that every Jedi, that the Jedi name is one that is respectable, regardless of fact the term comes from fiction. For too long the Jedi Community has allowed the Jedi name to be worthless. Not here. No more. We will not stand for it. We demand Jedi be a name you can take to the bank.

Lastly - I expect this exact level of accountability from you. No one is exempt, no one is untouchable, this triples for me and all leaders at the JAO. I will be there, I am there in the trenches, I give my time every day to the Jedi Path, to this site, and to the practices I mentioned above. It is my responsibility to be an example and you are encouraged to demand just as much (if not a lot more) from me as I do from you. If I act like a jackmonkey, I expect you to tell me so.

That said - and you are crazy enough to continue - once again Welcome to the Jedi Academy Online.

-= Introduction Assignment One =-

Part One:
Reflection Time. Reflect. Is this truly for you? Do you really want to be a Jedi? Do you have what it takes to find out? Reply in your journal whether you shall be staying or going. No shame in looking for something less blusterous, in something less demanding. Many Jedi sites that are very active and worth whatever time you can give them. If you want help looking for a place for you, just ask. We don't want you to give-up your search on the Jedi Lifestyle just because our style isn't a fit for you. From the Force Academy to the Real Jedi Enclave to the Temple of the Jedi Order, and others, many places to seek training. And we have first-hand knowledge of the type of atmosphere and training you'll received at such places.

Due As Soon As Possible. However - feel free to take the week to work through the lesson and see how it vibes with you. So a minute or a week - due as soon as you feel comfortable answering.

Part Two:
Incorporating Jedi Practices into Your Life - Daily.
NOTE: These are **not** to replace or be replaced by your current studies and activities. Meaning, if you already do a specific meditation, you are still to practice what is listed here. If you work-out and cover these exercises you are still to do them at some point. These are supplemental exercises for daily use, to be used in conjunction with your current lifestyle.

- Physical Fitness - Start with some light stretching (touch the toes, reaching for the sky, etc.). A little knee high marching in place. Now - Do 25 jumping jacks, 15 push-ups (knee push-ups allowed), 25 crunches (or sit-ups), and 15 squats. Daily, once is fine, any time, I recommend morning right when you get out of bed. Doesn't take me more than 5 minutes to complete.

•Meditation - I want you to just breathe. This will be your meditation for now. Just take a moment from time to time and just close your eyes and breathe deeply for a few moments. When in the shower, when waiting for something to load, in the morning before starting the morning routine, before bed, etc. Just take a moment and breathe.

•Awareness - Take a moment and just take in your surroundings. Above you, behind you, to the sides, below, just look around, note the things you see. To the left a wall with pictures, a smoke detector above me, window in front, beige house across the street. Do this when out for a walk, when you walk into a new room, go to the movies, etc. Do not try to catalog everything, do not take twenty minutes in the doorway looking at everything, just take the moment and note what you can. The things and people around you.

•Diplomacy - This one we are just going to focus more on listening to others. What is being said, the words used. How is it being said, the tone used. And not reacting either way to the words or tone, but instead focusing on meaning, the purpose. "Take out the dang garbage!" "Sure thing." Stop what you are doing, get it done. After a little time with that, you can start requesting a please. Seek to remove the emotion, and simply focus on what is truly being said and/or asked. And then act accordingly.

•Self-Discipline - This should be obvious. Just actually follow through on these practices daily. Incorporate them and keep them up for as long as you are in this program.

After the one week is up:
Give your personal thoughts on each point presented here. Your

general daily thoughts and reflections welcome. If you have not done so, start a journal in the the sub-forum (training journals) and turn in your assignment there. You are free to update throughout the week. All Due in One Week.

-===-

How to Perform the Exercises Listed:

Push-ups: How to Do It: Position yourself face down on the floor, balancing on your toes/knees and hands. Your hands should be wider than shoulders, body in a straight line from head to toe. Don't sag in the middle and don't stick your butt up in the air. Slowly bend your arms and lower your body to the floor, stopping when your elbows are at 90 degrees. Exhale and push back up.
Knee Push-ups: Same posture as described above, except wit your ankles crossed and your knees on the floor supporting your weight.

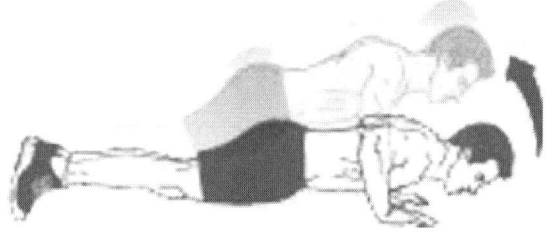

Sit-ups: If you can, use a ab machine, these are designed to help save your back by using proper posture. Outside that here is some tips on Crunches and proper technique. You may not know this, but many people do not use good form when doing an ab crunch. Not only can this cause back problems, it will also make your ab workout less effective. How to Do It:
-Lie down on the floor on your back and bend your knees, placing your hands behind your head or across your chest.
-Pull your belly button towards your spine, and flatten your lower back against the floor.
-Slowly contract your abdominals, bringing your shoulder blades about one or two inches off the floor.
-Exhale as you come up and keep your neck straight, chin up.

-Hold at the top of the movement for a few seconds, breathing continuously.
-Slowly lower back down, but don't relax all the way.
To add variation, bring your knees in at the same time you lift your upper body off the floor (full body crunch)
Tips:
To keep your neck in proper alignment, place your fist under your chin to keep your head from moving.
Keep your back flat against the floor throughout the entire movement.
If your back arches, prop your feet on a step or platform to make it easier.

Squats: How to Do it: Stand with feet hip-width apart, toes facing straight ahead or angled slightly outward. Slowly bend the knees and lower hips towards the floor, keeping your torso straight and abs pulled in tight. Keep your knees behind your toes; make sure everything's pointing in the same direction. Do not go lower than 90 degrees. (Form Pointers: Stand with feet shoulder-width apart. Slowly lower your body as though you are 'sitting' in a chair until your thighs are parallel with the ground. Keeping the weight in your heels, push yourself up slowly until you're back where you started. Key points: don't allow your knees to extend over your toes and keep your torso tight and erect.)

Introduction Lesson Part Two – Etiquette:

We will start with **Jedi Etiquette at the Jedi Academy Online.** Jedi are individuals who follow a set of rules. They find value in the structure and guidance. Likewise they acknowledge that while these rules and codes frame our actions, they do not hinder one from being an individual. They do not stop us from having our own traits, quirks, hobbies, likes, and dislikes. While we all follow the same path, that hardly makes us the same person.

Due to our varying personalities and the already difficult issues of online communication, there is room for misunderstanding and miscommunication. One of the ways we seek to avoid this is by following a simple code of conduct as well as using specific forms of address. In this we can all be on the same page and help work pass the pitfalls of communicating through our current medium.

Code of Conduct: Is a simple guideline to follow. One which you probably see just about in any formal place of teaching. Mutual Respect Policy - treat others how you would like to be treated. That is core, for all interactions, and an important part of diplomacy. More Flies with Honey - when in doubt be polite. We can joke with our friends, use our own brand of humor with those that know us, but being online it can be hard to convey proper tone and meaning. So seek to error on the side of caution. Don't Poop Where You Eat - In other words, treat this place with respect. No need for profanity. Online interactions afford us the time to chose our words. I cuss in-person, a bad habit I picked up in my younger days. Yet online I do not need to use that language. And it only serves to tarnish the academic environment of this place. Lastly, remember that people of all ages, all cultures, all beliefs, around the world visit this place. You set an example for all Jedi - uphold that responsibility accordingly.

Forms of Address: As written by Jaden. Navigating the perilous world of Jedi titles can be difficult. Thankfully, it is much easier at the Jedi Academy Online. Those of a lower Tier are of a lower rank, those of a higher Tier are of a higher rank. Rather then rely on Jedi Knight, Jedi Master, we look to acknowledge experience as living as a Jedi by denoting levels to it.

To formally address another Jedi, always refer to them as "Jedi ____". This is an easy rule that can be applied across the larger Jedi community, and means that you don't have to recognize the differences in titles such as "Knight" or "Master", which we don't have.

For Jedi of a higher rank, if you are unsure of another individual's placement in regards to you, or if you just wish to show greater respect, use their full name - for example "Jedi Opie Macleod". For a Jedi of lower rank, during a teaching session or formal meeting, you may refer to them simply by their last name - such as "Jedi Macleod." If the Jedi in question is using a one-word screen name, refer to them using the whole name - therefore "Jedi Delph" or "Jedi HappyTurtle." Whilst communicating with another, try to use the formal version until invited to use something more informal in order to avoid causing offense.

An Easy Example Guide:
- Jedi Opie Macleod (Formal - Highest form of Respect)
- Jedi Macleod (Formal - Respectful)
- Jedi Opie (Formal/Informal - Given Permission - Friendly)
- Opie (Intimate/Informal - Permission Only - High level of Friendship)

-= Introduction Assignment Two =-

1 - Read the Full JAO Code of Conduct. (Included in the back of the book. Included int eh conclusion chapter)
2 - In a formal setting what would be the proper way to use your name?
3 - What, during Tier One training, would you preferred to be called?
4 - A visitor to the JAO makes a post calling the Jedi stupid and

begins throwing out insults - acting outside our Code of Conduct policy. According to our Code of Conduct, does this behavior allow you to deviate from the Code of Conduct in order to deal with this individual? What does the Code of Conduct say on such matters? (Hint, you will need to complete #1 to get this.)
5 - Are you allowed to have Double-Accounts (two different accounts)? If so, why? If not, what stipulations might there be to that?
Due Today.

Introduction Lesson Part Three – Misconceptions:

There are a variety of misconceptions which exist about the Jedi Path. Calling yourself a Jedi is a big step, simply because it sounds so crazy. So first lets look at why anyone would bother to call themselves a Jedi. And to do that we must have a basic understanding of what the Jedi are in the fictional sense.

Jedi are a fictional Order in the Star Wars Universe created by George Lucas. Jedi are a variety of species and come from various cultures. This fictional order supports peace and justice in the galaxy. And serves, but is not a part of, the Republic (the galactic political system based upon democratic ideals). Jedi are not police or soldiers, but rather a highly respected order which people, governments, and planets can petition to help them out with various problems. Generally Jedi serve mostly as diplomats and mediators, seeking to reach fair and peaceful solutions.

Through the movies, books, and other media the Jedi have been role-models to many. An idea to aspire too. To be fair and just, helpful and supportive, skilled and respected. To be a Jedi, for many, is to be an individual who is wise, calm, in control, capable of handling the most hectic situations. Stalwart protectors of everything good in the world. Not a bad thing to try and aspire too, but the fact we all must face is that it is fictional. So how can we bridge the gap between fiction and reality, without losing touch of reality?

Fiction has been used to inspire many others over the years. From advanced and advancing technology to parables being used for centuries to help convey certain ideals. This is really no different. Star Wars inspired us and so this is the focus and terminology used. Wisdom can be found in many places, sometimes we see real life heroes who pass on their own wisdom. We also see that sometimes that wisdom comes from an author in a fictional tale. Either way we see the value, it speaks to us, and we seek to live our lives accordingly. We see something worth emulating and/or creating.

One of the things I recommend for people curious or new to the Jedi Path is to simply remove Jedi from the lessons. In some cases that is hard to do. But seek to look past the Star Wars terminology and determine if the ideals, the lessons themselves, hold any merit. Jedi is a title, a label, that we use for inspiration, for symbolism. You do not need to be a Star Wars fan to be a Jedi Knight, just have to find merit in living as a Jedi. And I truly feel most people can see the benefit, even if they do fully agree with the Path themselves.

In this, many feel that we could simply drop the Jedi name and focus and draw upon other philosophies, paths, and/or beliefs which already exist; such as Taoism. But the reason many of us have chosen the Jedi name is because it is not tied to a specific culture or Religion, giving us the freedom to believe what we want (or follow whatever religion or lack thereof we may choose). As well the Jedi's focus is much broader than most other established paths. Emotional, mental, physical, and spiritual well-being are all wrapped up and covered in one path. That is truly difficult to find in most Paths out there. You can find a focus on self-defense, but where is the core teaching of helping others? You can find focus on the spiritual, but where is the everyday practical application? You can find focus on emotional stability, but where is the focus on physical health? It is all left for us to piece together from this and that. And in doing such we never get a full and in-depth understanding of those great paths/beliefs out there.

So the Jedi focus on their path, finding the appeal in a broad focus, an all-encompassing ideal. No need to disrespect a path by doing it half way; no sense being a Zen-Christian-Stoic-Samurai. The Jedi Path is a complete journey of self-discovery and self-betterment. Which has religious freedom, meaning one can be a Christian, a Buddhist, Agnostic, Atheist, and still be a Jedi as well. But the best way to truly explain all this is to go through and show you the beginning steps of being a Jedi. Lets continue...

-= Introduction Assignment Three =-
What brought you to the Jedi Path? Why Jedi for You?
Who created Star Wars?
According to what is written above, do you need to be a Star Wars fan to live as a Jedi?
Due Today.

Introduction Lesson Part Four – Fiction-Based Reality:

Fiction Based Reality. This is what the Jedi are. We have taken from fiction, been inspired by fiction, and grown from fiction, all to affect and change our reality. And as crazy as it may seem, it does in fact work. This isn't much of a surprise considering that Jedi do not do anything that cannot be compared to somewhere path out there in the world. But certainly it can be confusing for some. How do we accomplish this? Why do we do it? Why not simply follow some other path with an established history?

This is what we are going to be looking at today. The reality of our path. First lets look at an example of how we do what we do. How we have spent over a decade applying fiction to reality and how it has proven to be a worthwhile endeavor. Fictional Ideal: "*You will know. When you are calm, at peace. Passive. A Jedi uses the Force for knowledge and defense, never for attack.*" - Yoda, Empire Strikes Back.

Here we have a simple quote, yet one which has resonated with many people. The question for Jedi becomes, how does this shape our views, lifestyle, and ideals, if at all? First step in breaking down the fiction is practical application. Can this be applied to our daily life in a practical sense? If yes, we must determine if it is indeed beneficial. Is this a positive addition to one's life? Does this allow for positive influence and effects not only within our own lives, but those around us as well?

This comes down to Doing. Experience. As Jedi we must find the answers ourselves. Fortunately for anyone new to the Jedi Path - a great deal of trial and error has already been done to weed out the useful from the completely fictional. Yet, lets see how this works, shall we?

How will you know good actions from bad actions? The fictional answer tells us when we are calm, at peace, passive. Can that possibly be true? Well, lets reflect. Think of a time when you acted impulsively. A time where you were upset, perhaps angry, and reacted without thought, but acted upon that turbulent emotional drive. Did it work out for you? Was the action beneficial? For all involved? In the long-term, short-term?

Most tend to give good advice when asked. Why? Because we are on the outside looking. We have a different view, a bird's eye understanding, where we can see many sides to the issue at hand. When we are faced with an issue that affects us personally, we get tunnel vision, we see only what is ahead of us, and often do not consider the many other sides and options within the situation. This is basic human nature and not something I'd label as bad, but again human nature is to label negative outcomes as bad. Personally, I see it all as experience and a learning opportunity.

But here we can start to see the value of this quote. It is about stopping, even if just for a half-a-second, and seeking that calm passive view. Finding that peace within ourselves and addressing our problems with that same clarity which we can advise others. Of course, as all things, much easier said than done. But this is why no one is a Jedi in a day, or a month, but it takes years to turn Human Nature into Jedi Nature. Making our actions and practices become that second-nature reflex we desire.

When growing up, I had a hard time with this quote. I was impulsive, reckless, I reacted within the moment, guided only by my emotions. It was a night and day difference when this began to sink-in. I was able to stop those horrible choices. Choices that led me to pack up and move across states leaving a good job with no job security or financial security. Which ultimately lead to broken friendships and poor romantic relationships.

By applying this simple concept I am able to take that step back. See the problems, see the solutions to the problem, and much more willing to take my time to resolve them. Without the emotional drive clouding my actions. Rather when at peace, I am able to realize what those emotional responses are seeking to tell me and how they relate to the overall situation and myself. They become tools of information rather than motivators of reckless actions.

      I do not expect you to take my word for it however. Like all of the Jedi Path - experience speaks much louder than any rambling on my part. So, lets explore this concept more. We will take the next three days and seek to incorporate this ideal into our lives and see if we we can't build on the what is presented here. And if you need more time, take it to the end of Tier One. Fully bring it into your life. Here are your assignments.

-= Introduction Assignment Four =-

1.) Do you feel the fictional quote, *"training to become a Jedi is not an easy task. And even if you succeed it is a hard life."* is applicable to us or completely fictional? Why?
Due Today.

2.) Calm, at Peace, Passive. Your mantra for the next three days. Before making a decision, take a deep breath and say it (in your head is fine). Seek to embody the ideal, if only for the brief decision-making second. Starting right now and ending when this lesson ends (though if you enjoy it - keep it up, no reason to stop a Jedi practice just because a lesson is over. Remember being a Jedi is a life-long journey).

At the end of the three days left (in tier one) - speak on your experience using this. Did it help? Did you find the ideal beneficial to your life? Do you feel this fictional concept is applicable, in a practical sense, to your everyday life? Share your thoughts.
Due in Three Days.

Introduction Lesson Part Five – JAO History:

As you have given your time and effort to the Jedi Academy Online I figure it would be nice to give you some history to this particular group. I find history to be a core part of learning. This is something you will find in all your future lessons. History to the subjects and lessons within the Jedi Community. Not only will you learn about the Jedi Code, but you will learn its history, how it has evolved within the Jedi Community, and where we are current at. In this you can understand where we have been and why things are the way they are.

This is no different. In the Jedi Community there are several groups and sites that you can participate in. From the Institute of Jedi Realist Studies to the Force Academy to the Temple of the Jedi Order there is a plethora places you can explore the Jedi Path. Each offers a unique experience and perspective. This is easily tied to the history of the particular site and the history of the site creators. So to better understand why the Jedi Academy Online takes the approach it does here is a brief history.

The Jedi Academy Online was originally created in 2007 by myself, Opie Macleod. I had created the site after a website I had created for myself called the Jedi Path began to get members who were interested in training in the material presented. This was not the first site creation venture for me. In fact my very first Jedi site I created was in 2000 under the name Followers of the Force. I later changed the name in 2001 to The Jedi Resource Center with a change of focus. This site was built on homestead with forums on ez-board, both which have been lost to time and the evolution of the internet.

My own history is a long one and would be worth a book by itself. Yet it is important to understand the mindset that built this place, the how and why it was created. This may get a bit long and meh, but I ask to stick with it. But if not, I'll be nice - here is the Short Version:

I was disillusioned with the Jedi Community. My dreams had been stomped on my a bunch of people who I felt only cared about an online club of fake titles. So in 2006 I created the Jedi Path (after some other failed attempts) website to explore my own training. By 2007 people had expressed an interest in joining in and being a part of it. That liked what they saw and wanted more. In March 2007 the Jedi Academy Online was born. To offer what no other site did, to be a place where the Jedi Circle was taught in-depth.

For the past five years we have excelled in this endeavor. And while we have changed several times in the academy, format, and style, one thing has always remained the same; we have always presented the Jedi Circle as the core way to live as a Jedi in everyday life. Currently there are no signs of us stopping any time soon. People see value in the Jedi Philosophy and seek a calm place they can pursue the study of the Jedi Path with complete focus. That is the Jedi Academy Online.

Long (Ramblely) Version:

I have been a part of the online Jedi Community (fully active) since 1999 (I lurked and watched since 1996). In that time I have been a part of many projects, many websites, and have earned a lot of titles (such as Knight, Councilor, etc.). Yet while I recognized I earned them per the site, going through the training programs and such, I personally never felt I achieved them by my own standards. This began years of fighting against popular notions in the Jedi Community. At one time labels such as Grey Jedi, Blue Jedi, Forest Jedi, Water Jedi, etc. existed in number and were very popular. I found myself at odds debating against such labels. This would become a trend with standards, with administration control, with who sites were run, with online training, with ideas of Jedi application, the most recent was with labels such as Jediism and Jedi Realism. Constantly I stood against popular practices in our online Community. And while I wasn't always alone in my views, constantly I lost those battles. As such the Jedi Community continued on moving in one direction while I and a few others were moving in another.

Time sorted out the issues in time. No longer are labels such as Blue or Red Jedi used or accepted. Standards have evolved. No longer is three months and an online written test acceptable for Knighthood. All sites now carry a code of conduct, by-laws, and have core rules and regulations in site management. And if I had stood in my footprints since 2001 then the Jedi Community and I would be perfectly happy together - on the same page. However constant growth is core to being a Jedi. I have never met an actual Jedi who is satisfied with how things are, they are always looking to learn more, be more, gain more, they are in a constant state of progress. Tearing down the old lessons and building new ones from them.

So I found myself without a Jedi website/group that I felt comfortable with dedicating myself too. I spent a lot of time and effort into a group called JEDI originally the Jedi Organization which evolved out the original Jedi United. In 2005 it had been handed over to the members. And it was quickly dying out. The creator, Relan Volkum, granted my request to allow me to have administration control and seek to turn it around. This unfortunately only lead to a centralized clash of ideals. A singular place and moment that summed up my entire Jedi career previously - fighting against the majority who had no desire to grow or change. JEDI went under and I lost my own desire to associate with the Jedi Community.

I had just created the Jedi Circle or then labeled the Circle of the Jedi. If you haven't read it, you can find a copy posted at the top of the Courtyard forum. Anyhow, I had a singular student who enjoyed it and wanted to learn more on it and about it. So I decided to create my own place for us to explore and work together to rebuild our foundation as Jedi with the Jedi Circle as our core. I went through a couple websites eventually settling on the Jedi Path, which as mentioned gained a small following. And thus the Jedi Academy Online was born March 2007.

For the past five years (at this time of writing) it has been under constant change. There has not been one year where there hasn't been changes to the Academy, to the lessons, and to the site itself. In fact I do not believe there has even been a six months period where at least one of those wasn't changed. This place is meant to be the embodiment of the Jedi Ideals. Determination, Constant Growth, Openness, Helping Others to Help Themselves, Service.

The Jedi Academy Online changed its name briefly to the Jedi Foundation. This was due to a change in focus briefly. Seeking to become a big organization which had several focuses. However, this once again showed that the Jedi Community as a whole is simply not there yet. It is still tribal and clings to its differences rather than its similarities. So instead of fighting it, we embraced it.

Our little tribe in the Jedi Community is the JAO. It offers a place where isms do not exist. Where segregation is a misconception and our individual diversity is embraced. It is a place that says anyone can be a Jedi if they are willing to work hard enough. It is a place that demands if one carries the Jedi that they truly live it, that they meet the standards of such a title. It is a place that focuses on practical application. It is a place that focuses on applying Jedi Philosophy to everyday life. It is a place that believes being a Jedi is a 365 lifestyle that makes no demands on your religious or spiritual outlook, only that your spiritual well-being is healthy. It is a place that says the Jedi Path is about your Physical, Mental, Emotional, Spiritual, and Social Well-Being. It is about World-Betterment via Self-Betterment. Not lightsabers, not magical powers, but hard work and self-improvement.

For over a decade I have sought a place that is about honest growth, a loyal community, and a commitment and caring for living as Jedi. For the past five years the Jedi Academy Online has been that place and surprisingly enough not just for me. We seek to ensure we have a fair, honest, caring, loyal, place dedicated to the Jedi Ideals. We seek a calm and focused atmosphere on not just being Jedi, but living it on a daily basis. How it reflects in all the little things we do.

-= Introduction Assignment Five =-

Explore a little Jedi History:
Look through this site created in 2001. While this version was actually used in 2006, the material is the same as the 2001 version. This version is simply easier to navigate.
This site is called the Real Jedi Knights. It was created in 2001 by Mi-Zhe Fu. I offer this as a comparison of evolution and growth in our community. As this this site very much embodied the mindset of the early Jedi. While 2001 was a year of extreme growth in our Community, this best shows the view points of many Jedi had at the time and before. It also offers a very clear comparison for the JAO and I want you to get a feel for the different styles and outlooks within the greater Jedi Community.
- **Archived Real Jedi Knights Website –** You can find a link written out at the back of the book.

Q&A Time:
First, if you haven't updated us on how the practices and study has been going. Please do so. Remember, all questions, comments, concerns are welcome. The more you engage us, the more we can engage you and that way we can give better feedback.

Second - What are your initial thoughts on the Real Jedi Knights? Do you feel there truly has been areas of growth in the way we approach the Jedi Path? Is the Real Jedi Knights more what you were expecting and/or wanting? Which style do you prefer more? Which style do you feel best represents the Jedi Path?
Due Today.

Introduction Lesson - Day Seven:

You have a couple assignments due. In the first assignment, you were asked if this was for you. A minute or a week, due whenever you feel comfortable. Yet I given the week, the practices, the assignments, the feedback, et cetera, do you feel this is indeed something you want to continue with?
You also have another assignment due today, but no hints from me on which one. Also - don't get to use to reminders. They won't always come and only one person will be held accountable (hint, it isn't me).

Lesson One – The Jedi Code:
The Misconception of the Code

The Jedi Code:
There is no emotion; there is peace.
There is no ignorance; there is knowledge.
There is no passion; there is serenity.
There is no chaos; there is harmony.
There is no death; there is the Force.

Before I get into the meat and potatoes of the Jedi Code there is something I want to speak on. That is the misconception that comes with the Code, with the Jedi Path in general (due to the Jedi Code). Experiencing Life.

There is no emotion - There is no ignorance - There is no passion - There is no chaos - There is no death. To many people the Jedi ideals conveyed here denounce some of the core aspects of life. Fear of death pushes us to live. Ignorance allows us to make new discoveries and explore the unknown. Passion fans the fires of life, giving us direction and pursuit. Emotions fill one with all the flavors of life. Chaos proves the unexpected, it makes life interesting. Many feel that to deny these things is to deny life itself. The beauty, joy, and greatness which is life.

I am one that values experience. I value it in all states. Meaning I do value the experience of others, as well as the experience of myself. While I do not enjoy going through rough times, the experience is something I find useful and valuable. Where one labels it good or bad or a mixture of everything I find nearly all experiences to provide something worthwhile.

No one has been, will be, or is born a Jedi. We all come to this path for our own reasons. We all have life experiences which we bring with us. We have all been angry, sad, afraid, happy. Some of us have been deeply in love, some only think they have been in love, and some are still searching for love. We all have experiences which we can label good or bad. In this, no Jedi comes to the Jedi Path without a core understanding of what it means to simply be human. And all the positives and negatives we associate with that.

Yet the Jedi Code is not putting an end to that. The Jedi Path is not stopping one from experiencing life. This isn't about suppression, it is not about ignoring, it is not about following the Jedi Code literally. That is not the Jedi Way. The Jedi Path is much more than that, it is much more than control and removal. In fact the Jedi Code and the Jedi Path is very much about experiencing all of life. Feeling all of it, being in the thick of it. The only difference is the Jedi Code is telling us not to be overcome by life. Experience it in all ways, but do not be overcome by it, do not be ruled by it. Be like the surfer, ride the wave, in touch with the wave but capable and free to change your direction at any time.

If I impart one thing in this lesson (which I will harp on over and over) it is that the Jedi Code is not a literal strict rule for the Jedi. It is a path, it is a direction, it is a reminder of how to live as a Jedi. It is not lack of emotion (passion, etc.), it is not suppression, it is not even control. It is stability, it is oneness, it is harmony, it is flowing with life without being ruled by life.

I can type, speak, lecture, until we both die of boredom. The only way to fully understand this is experiencing it. Experiencing all sides of this. So for the next week will we continually examine the Jedi Code, use it as a mantra and meditation, we will apply it and see what conclusions we come to. I'd like you, from this point forward, to allow the Jedi Code to be your guide and core to the Jedi Path, to Jedi Philosophy.
On to the weekly practices...

-= Lesson One Assignment One =-
Incorporating Jedi Practices into Your Life - Daily. Part Two
NOTE: <u>These are not to replace or be replaced by your current studies and activities</u>. Meaning, if you already do a specific meditation, you are still to practice what is listed here. If you

work-out and cover these exercises you are still to do them at some point. These are supplemental exercises for daily use, to be used in conjunction with your current lifestyle.

•Physical Fitness - Start with some light stretching (touch the toes, reaching for the sky, etc.). A little knee high marching in place. Now - Do 10 Lunges (both legs: right + left = 1), 10 Leg Raise Push-ups (5 each leg), 15 Squat Thrusts, 10 Mountain Climbers (right + left = 1), 20 V-ups, and 20 Squats. Daily, Once, any time; I recommend morning right when you get out of bed. Doesn't take me more than 10 minutes to complete (seven minute is my average time). Pictures At the End. As a side-note, you can rest, mid-set break, but accomplish the numbers given. Those sit-ups can wear you out.

•Meditation - Last week we focused on breathing. This time around we are going to add the Jedi Code as a mantra. I want you to take a few moments in the morning, in the evening, at lunch, sit, observe (or close your eyes), breathe as before and this time repeat the Jedi Code 3 to five times. Do this if feeling stressed, head to the bathroom to get some alone time if needed.
Also seek to apply and use a line as needed. If you are having an emotional moment and need to make a decision, beforehand repeat that line - *There is no emotion; there is peace* a few times before pressing forward. Told to learn something new (which you may not want too or think you know already) - *There is no ignorance; there is knowledge* a few times before proceeding. So on and so forth.

•Awareness - Last week we focused on outward awareness. Picking up on the things and people around you. Be aware of your surroundings. And still keep that habit up. It is good to have. However, this time we are going to focus on inward Awareness. Being aware of the Self. Of what is going on inside our minds and body. I want to really take note of what is going on inside that body of yours.

Time to be your own little therapist. Ask yourself - why do I feel this way? Why did I react like that? How does this make me feel? This extends not just to the mental and emotional, but the physical as well. How does you body feel? Do you feel physically different when you feel emotionally different? How does your mood effect you overall?

• <u>Diplomacy</u> - Last week - removal of tone. Focusing on what is being said/asked, not the how. This helps us in understanding that in diplomatic situations, we have to remove the ego and focus on the issues, the problems at hand. This time we are going to flip it a bit at us. I want you to focus on your own tone. Take full accountability of your tone, the way you say things, and how you ask for things.

Work on the general politeness, Please, Thank you, I appreciate it. Even when cheesed-off, I want you to note your tone of voice. You are fully responsibility during this time for how people take your comments and questions. Mad at something else? No excuse for answering someone or the phone in an upset manner. Full responsibility.

• <u>Self-Discipline</u> - This should be obvious. Just actually follow through on these practices daily. Incorporate them and keep them up for as long as you are in this program. Hey something that didn't change. Congrats! Now - Go Live as a Jedi. Apply apply apply - no just learning, no just knowing, DO!

Today's Assignment:
Have you ever felt fear, happiness, anger, and sadness at some point in your life? If yes, I want you to think of a time/situation that brought forth one or more of these feelings (you do not have

to share them, just think of them).
If you could, would you erase those experiences from your life? Did you ultimately learn from those experiences? Do you feel there is anything more to be learned from them?
Do you believe there is value in feeling emotions and having passion? What of ignorance, experiencing chaos? Do you feel death is a necessary part of life? To all these questions (whether yes or no) why?
Due Today.

Exercise Pictures:
Lunges: Stand comfortably, extend one leg forward, bending at the knee. Do Not let your other knee hit the ground. Stand back up, alternate legs.

Push-up with Leg Raise: Same as a normal push-up, with the addition, that when in the up position you bring one knee into your chest. Put it back, then down, up, other knee into chest.

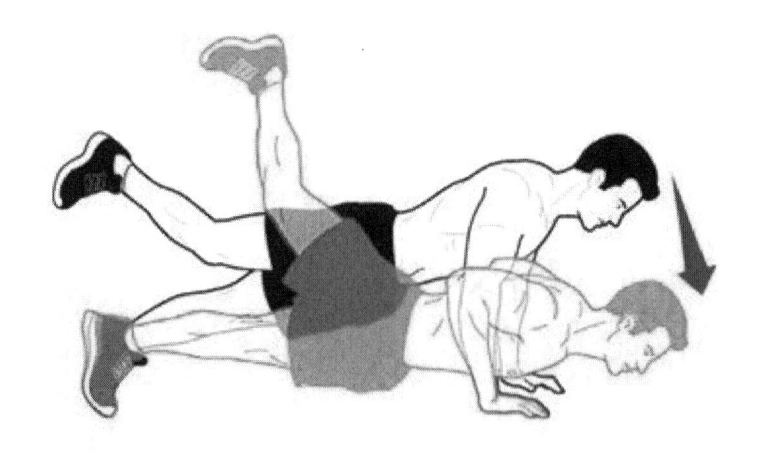

Squat Thrusts: Stand up straight. Squat down, kick your feet out so you are in the Push-up position. Bring your feet back in. Stand up. (A Burpee is the same movement, but adds in a push-up while in that position. Just as an FYI)

Mountain Climbers: Get into the starting Push-up Position. Now, you push off with your leg, bring the knee into the chest, while the other leg stays extended. Kick your leg back and bring the other knee into the chest.

V Sit-ups: Lay on your back, flat on the ground. Arms extended above your head. Legs out straight. Bring your arms over and in front of you, reaching toward your toes. At the same time lift your legs up. And bringing your shoulders and back off the floor. Lay back down bringing your arms back over your head.

Squats: Stand with feet hip-width apart, toes facing straight ahead or angled slightly outward. Slowly bend the knees and lower hips towards the floor, keeping your torso straight and abs pulled in tight. Keep your knees behind your toes; make sure everything's pointing in the same direction. Do not go lower than 90 degrees.

The Jedi Code - Day Two:
The Jedi Code Overview - Learning the Code.

The first step to understanding the Jedi Path is understanding the very core that drives it. In 1980 the Empire Strikes Back came out and this really established a love for the Jedi. This old crazy hermit who turns out to be wise helps train the hero Luke Skywalker in his journey to become a Jedi Knight like his father before him. This is where many felt their first connection to walking the path of the Jedi. The words and ideas said within the movie simply spoke to people.

In 1987 the first published version of the Jedi Code was released. It was released for the Star Wars tabletop role-playing game. When looking at this original version of the Jedi Code fans of the movies can see where the ideals sprang from - the lines from Empire which inspired the ideals presented within the Jedi Code. These were not new concepts, George Lucas did not create new ideas, but expanded and combined preexisting ideals. The authors who wrote the Jedi Code also sought outside influence in their creation. It was this simple text which would become the bedrock of the Jedi Path and Jedi Community.

It was been well over twenty years since the Jedi Code first appeared. As one would expect there have been changes, new versions, and different takes on the Code. Not only within the Star Wars fiction, but also as the Jedi Community grew so did our understanding of the Jedi Code. So while authors of fiction sought to alter and change the Jedi Code, so did those following the Path seek to create a better version of the Jedi Code. There are currently three major versions which are called the Jedi Code, all which have their home/origin in the fiction.

The Original Jedi Code - per 1987:
There is no emotion; there is peace.
There is no ignorance; there is knowledge.

There is no passion; there is serenity.
There is no death; there is the Force.

The Five Line Jedi Code - created in 1996:
Emotion, yet peace.
Ignorance, yet knowledge.
Passion, yet serenity.
Chaos, yet harmony.
Death, yet the Force.

What we will be using here at the Jedi Academy Online is a combination of the two which was used by BioWare in their 2002 hit game Knights of the Old Republic. It uses the format of the first, but the lines of the second. It is as follows:
There is no emotion; there is peace.
There is no ignorance; there is knowledge.
There is no passion; there is serenity.
There is no chaos; there is harmony.
There is no death; there is the Force.

This is what we will be referring to when we say the Jedi Code. There are other texts which have been labeled the Jedi Code, such as the Jedi Creed and the Jedi Rules of Behavior. We will look at these briefly and explain them in the days to come. For now this five line Code is what will be our basis. Learn it, memorize it, let it become your mantra. This is the core element of our Path and has been since the Jedi Community first started. For over 13 years this Code has been at the heart of every single person who call themselves a Jedi. It is what has helped many Jedi through tough situations and gain clarity when they felt lost.

The questions we come too are how, why, what does it mean, is it literal. These are concerns which many have. They look at the Jedi Code and they see that first part. There is no emotion, there is no passion, what is life if we do not experience these core factors in being alive? This is a valid question and the first thing we are going to tackle.

The Jedi Code is not a set of literal rules in which one must live their life. The Jedi Code is an ideal, it is a reflection upon human behavior, as well as a homage to the original Star Wars trilogy. The view and use of the Jedi Code in actual life has evolved over the years. Currently you will find that most Jedi use the Jedi Code as a mantra, a reminder, a way to help them put their actions into perspective. Jedi use the Jedi Code to help them temper their actions and reactions, reminding themselves that to be blinded by emotion, ignorance, passion, chaos, or even death rarely resolves our issues in a positive/beneficial manner.

One of the ways I use to teach the proper use of the Jedi Code was to see first-hand the difficulty, the absurdity, the negative impact following the Jedi Code literally had. One would seek to live it literally for two weeks. Naturally this was not a wisest technique, a little too much like sticking your hand in the fire to learn fire burns. Combined with the fact that one doesn't really see the long-term damage done, the suppression of emotion that arises. The fact that would would need to be a sociopath to truly follow it literally. It breeds apathy and stagnation sucking the very element of life out of every moment.

When I started the Jedi Path I was a child, literally. There was no internet to me to access and I had no mentors, guides, or teachers. I had a role-playing book and three movies. I look the Jedi Code at face-value, I sought to live it faithfully and literally. What I learned from that experience was the perfect what-not-to-do. When I eventually came to the Jedi Community I fought against the open and loose interpretation of the Jedi Code. I had spent years of my life fighting to uphold the Code in a literal sense. Eventually, through that trial and error, through exploring other ideals, and through the experiences life threw my way I was able to see the damage I had caused to myself. As we get to know each other I may share my own specific experiences as well as the experiences of others I have heard over the years which highlight this point.

One thing which will always come up is that the Jedi Path is a lifestyle of Physical, Mental, Emotional, Spiritual, and Social

Well-Being. The Jedi Code in a literal sense harms the emotional and even social well-being of the individual following it. And this is a major reason why we start out with the Jedi Code as the first lesson. It teaches to major elements which are recurring themes throughout one's life as a Jedi.

The first being the core ideals of the Jedi. Peace, Knowledge, Serenity, Harmony, and the Force. Which is something we will be exploring throughout the week. Looking at each concept and how it applies to our life. Which brings us to point number two. The fact that we acknowledge our inspiration, our material for personal growth, is in fact born of fiction. As such we must not take everything at face-value. A lot of what we teach, of what we show, of what we live is from the years upon years of trial and error. It is based upon the experience of Jedi living as Jedi. Finding out what is applicable to our everyday lives and what is simply fiction or even harmful to our daily lives.

-= Jedi Code Main Assignment =-

For this first main assignment I want you to examine the Jedi Code. Learn it inside and out. I want you to reflect daily on the Jedi Code and how it relates to your life, how it governs your life, if at all. Keep it in mind, memorize it, at the day of the end weigh your day against it. You are going to be doing this for One Week. Seven full days of reflection. You need not report here on it, unless you want to, unless you have questions or desire some feedback. At the end of the Week however, you will be asked your views, thoughts, interpretation, and experience with the Jedi Code. This will be your main/final assignment and will ultimately determine if you move onto the next lesson. Forewarned is forearmed, I will expect your assignment to reflect a week's worth of study and application.

-= Day Two Assignment =-

1.) Which Star Wars movie seems to have the most influence on the Jedi Code?
2.) Which line in the Code speaks to you? Any one in particular?

None, all? Any reason why?
3.) Out of the three versions written above which is your favorite? The 2002 long five line code the JAO uses or the 1996 short five line version? Why is that? Simply the way it sounds, the way it looks, the flow to the words? Why that version?
Due Today.

The Jedi Code - Day Three through Seven:
Application of the Jedi Code (line by line) -

Like many things in life and all Jedi lessons there is a difference between studying and applying. A difference between knowing and doing. I do not want you to just know the Jedi Code or Jedi Philosophy in general, I want you to live it. In this it is important that we examine the Jedi Code, that we understand it, and know it, but it is vital for a Jedi to apply it, to live it. Yet as discussed previously there are proper ways to go about applying the Code and improper ways. Trying to literally apply the Code can hurt one's emotional well-being, as we do not want to repress or bottle up what and how we feel. We simply want to process it differently. So we will be look at each line and taking some everyday examples into consideration. Examining how Jedi have and do apply the Jedi Code to their daily lives.

A Jedi once told me that "*to Know and to Act are one and the same.*" When you know what you are suppose to do you will in fact do it. This is a great theory, but ultimately one I have found to be completely false. How many times have you heard or even said, "*I know*" when being admonish for a mistake or improper behavior? Many times we know, and our hindsight vision is 20/20. After-the-fact we often clearly see and know exactly what we did wrong and do not understand why we didn't do what we knew (even at the time) to be the proper action.

As Jedi we are going to seek to close that gap. We are going to make that quote a reality. To know and to act to be one and the same for us. Yet how can we do that? By providing a framework. By gaining not just knowledge, but understanding. Not just understanding, but examples of application. Each day we will look at one line of the Jedi Code.

Now to be clear - this is a tier one introduction program. Each of these topics will be explored much more in-depth as one progresses through the training. We touch on Emotional Wellness, Mental/Intellectual Wellness, et cetera, yet we do not fully dive into the topics completely until later Tiers. Keep this in mind. We are simply seeking to build the foundations of Jedi Thought and Lifestyle here.

This is the beginning steps into the Jedi lifestyle. This is not the end all be all. Thus I highly recommend seeking your own studies on the application of ideas presented here. Unfortunately we do not have the resources to make all that available to you - even in the later tiers. A lot of Jedi study and application is going to fall on your shoulders alone. As we unfortunately do not have Jedi Masters to watch over you in your daily life, like the fiction, either. So understand this is bare minimum basics.

That said - lets get to it.

The Jedi Code - Day Three:
Line One: Emotional Stability

There is no emotion; there is peace.

For ten years Jedi in the Jedi Community have decreed this a line of Emotional Control. I disagree. I say it is a line of Emotional Stability. We, as Jedi, should feel, acknowledge, and experience our emotions as any other. Anger, fear, happiness, sorrow, whatever the case may be. We should easily be able to say to people "Yes, I am a bit scared." or "I am sorry, I am really angry right now, so I need some time before I make that decision." And these should be said in very matter-of-fact tones. Acknowledging what and how we feel without them completely taking us for a ride.

No one can shorten my fuse quicker than my Mother. The key here is expectations. Standards. What we expect and hold others to. Most people I have a rather low expectation of. Which is great because I am pleasantly surprised at times. However when people don't reach those expectations is when we find ourselves getting upset with them and even ourselves. I get frustrated at times with my Mother because of the expectations I have, which aren't always fair.

Yet, the key to the this line of the Code is in being stable in that. Meaning, it isn't found in not getting upset, but rather when upset not allowing that to interfere with judgment, understanding, consideration, forethought, afterthought, etc. Being stressed, mad, hurt, sad, tired, hungry, these are not excuses for unJedi-like behavior. these are daily occurrences that happen to us all. Yet we are still Jedi and still held - regardless - to those ideals and this lifestyle.

So when I feel upset - I feel it, but is does not bother me, it does not affect me, it does not alter my course, tone, views, actions. It is felt, it is acknowledged, and it continues on its way. I am stable, I am fluid, yes I can note that I am upset without showing signs that people tend to associate with being upset. I can make note of it without having it actually affect my demeanor. This is the essence of the first line of the Jedi Code - feel, but don't be controlled, acknowledge, but do not give-into, experience the emotion, but do not act on it.

    The difference between Control and Stability is simply Need. When I feel angry I do not feel the need to act on it. This is stability. I am at peace with my emotions. They do not incite a desire to react.

    Make no mistake - in these first steps, in the beginning of the journey, when I first began, control was necessary. I use to be very angry. Punching walls, breaking things, I had that knee-jerk reaction as a teenager to act on what I felt. I, like many of you, needed restraint, control, I had to stop myself from acting. But that is not what the Code is telling us - that is not the end of the line for Jedi - that is the healthy way to live.

    Example - ever get mad at an electronic? When I was younger - I have had a few computer screens broken. Control gave way to emotion. Anger built up - released and bam! Sore knuckles and broken for good electronics. Not good on any level. Not smart on any level. And certainly not Jedi on any level. Electronics being what they are I have had my share of chances to revisit this scenario time and again. At first control was mandatory. The anger was there, the fist clenched, but recited the Code, retained control, acting in anger avoided. A Jedi Step/Level One Accomplishment. But as you grow as a Jedi, as I did, the need to act diminishes. The realization and truth of it becomes second-nature or really just becomes first-nature. What does it solve?

    In time you see that acting emotionally doesn't resolve issues as you want, hoped, or need. Sure you still feel the emotion, but are aware on every level that acting upon it solves nothing and only offers immediate temporary personal relief. Thus, you feel the emotion, but not the need to act. It is a progression. This is the ultimate goal of the Jedi Code - to offer the understanding that while we experience emotion it is not emotion that rules us.

It is a process, it is a tool, but it is one that we must seek to remove in time. And if I can do it, truly anyone is capable of it. So yes, you will need to control yourself at first, but always, from day one, seek Stability, feeling without control, acknowledging without action. Do not let the emotion dictate your actions - rather allow the emotion to simply help you understand the situation and yourself.

Stability is about accepting and learning from the experience without judgment. Observing without labeling. Feeling without acting. It is about coming to terms with the whole of life. You will feel emotions on a daily basis and that is not a bad thing. Emotions are indicators, pointing to things we should take note of. Emotions aren't to be ignored, or bottled, or shoved away. Acknowledge, Accept, Allow. Emotion isn't the enemy. We alone, regardless of how we feel, are responsible for our actions.

Now I personally do not count stress as an emotion. Yet certainly when we are stressed we are much more inclined to emotions, emotional behavior, and acting on those emotions. A key part of emotional stability is stress management. Which ultimately comes down to good time management and having a good stress reliever. Be it video game, physical game (racket-ball, basketball, etc.), Martial Arts, Boxing, Trail Running, Hot Bubble Bath, good book, all of the above, whatever it may be; simply find something that allows you to find that peaceful center within and let go of all that stress.

-= Day 3 Assignment =-

Finding the Proper Release of Emotion (de-stresser)
- What is your preferred de-stressing method? What returns you to sanity?
Paying Attention?
- According to above, what is the difference between Control and Stability? Explain, in your own words.
Expressing Emotion Properly
- What is the best method for expressing that you are angry? Be

as detailed as possible.
All Due by Tomorrow.

The Jedi Code - Day Four:
Line Two: Know Thy Self

     Before I begin my own rambling on this line "**There is no ignorance; there is knowledge.**" I want to share the section on this concept from the Power of the Jedi sourcebook. It really says all one needs, but that won't stop me from boring you with my writing anyhow. Still it offers a great view to understand what the line means. Please keep in mind that this is a fictional source meant for fictional Jedi - so it may seem a bit extreme at times.
Quote

Ignorance kills as surely as anger. A little knowledge might be dangerous, but a lack of knowledge is deadly. Ignorance of others, ignorance of facts, and ignorance of truth sets individuals apart and leads to contention and violence. A Jedi spreads knowledge that unifies, binding peoples and worlds together.

This knowledge begins with the Jedi knowing their own capabilities, strengths, and weaknesses. Pride can cloud the mind and make them blind to their own flaws, which might be exploited by others. Failure cause doubt, which causes the Jedi to be less capable of realizing their own strengths. Jedi continually test themselves to see where the limits of their abilities lie, not as a goal in itself, but as a means to the goal of better understanding themselves.

Within a Jedi campaign, challenging the Jedi's knowledge may be as simple as unraveling a mystery or as deep as forcing Jedi to understand their own limitations. Those who oppose the Jedi and their beliefs move in the shadows and fear revelation in the light. By the same token, the Jedi must always be vigilant of their own nature, seeking out weaknesses in the soul and spirit and rising to overcome them.

Tough to follow that. What more is there to say? Being a Jedi is about the path of knowledge. Self-Knowledge, Occupational Knowledge, General Knowledge, Preserving Knowledge, Respecting Knowledge, Seeking Knowledge. What cannot be solved with the right knowledge? What cannot be overcome with the proper know how?

Knowledge is Power - Power is Change.
The Jedi Path is about gaining control over You. So that you may in turn gain control over your world and thus affect world change (even on a global scale). Never underestimate the power of a singular human in full control of their own destiny. And what are you? You darn right - a human being gaining full control of your life, your fate, your future.

Chance? Please, not even close. Knowledge. Information. Experience. As Jedi we develop ourselves via knowledge. It gives us the power to make changes. The more knowledge, the more power, the more power, the more responsibility (use whatever favorite superhero quote you want on that). This is the beauty, challenge, strength in the Jedi Path. To not turn away from knowledge, even the tough to swallow stuff we'd rather not face.

It is about facing ourselves, facing hard truths, it is in overcoming short-comings in us, in our abilities, in our world, in the world in general. There will be times we are faced with obstacles, with hard choices, with situations that scream run and hide in a hole all alone. Yet it is knowledge that battles this instinct. The knowledge we can and will make a difference. The knowledge that we are strong creatures, even if we need a reminder from those close to us. The knowledge that we will bounce back no matter the dark times we face, no matter the weight crushing us, we will survive, we will live to rise another day, and turn the tables by gaining control of life.

It is here we see the mix of being a Jedi. Yesterday all about Emotional Stability. Not Control, but Stability. And this is the goal emotional goal for Jedi. To feel, to experience the richness of life, the high and the lows, but to gain a stability within that crazy ride. Achievable by all, yet here we see the focus on Control. The idea that we have the power, the ability, to control our environment, to control our lives, our direction, our focus, our fate. It may seem complex at first, given a little time, understanding wins the day and you will see the wonderful simplicity of it all.

Today we will use Self-Knowledge as the basis. It is this knowledge that will serve you the best in life. In all walks, areas, careers of life. Self-Knowledge is the most important and can very much help make up for lack of knowledge in other areas. So that is where our assignment will be today. And I hope I have imparted the importance of this aspect of the Jedi for the rest of your life, Jedi or not. Know Thy Self indeed.

-= Day 4 Assignment =-

Time to face inward, examine and write out You. Please take a moment to relax, to center yourself, and be ready to reflect on the self. For this exercise I want you to fill in where I leave off. But I want to stress, two things. One, be completely honest. Two, you are just starting out (presumably) as a Jedi, don't feel you have to have an answer, or even a "*Jedi answer*". Just be honest. We will look at this later on down the line and see what changes may have taken place during your time and training as a Jedi here. This is for you, not to impress anyone.

I am
I share
I express
I build
I change
I comfort
I seek
I accumulate
I feel
I accept

I expand
We are
Due by Tomorrow.

The Jedi Code - Day Five:
Line Three: Calm Center

There is no passion; there is serenity. Tough line - mostly because it belies a lot of concepts. Unlike the previous two it is not about control and it is not about stability. It is about understanding the differences in extremes. It is about finding the benefits in two worlds and arriving at the proper area in both places. This is about ensuring balance in two very separate topics.

Passion is essential to a fruitful life. Any museum or observatory or like building will show the value of passion. You think this website would exist without passion? My passion for the Jedi Path is what demands this place and the constant improvements. Passion is simply one of the many great spices of life. Yet we can see passion placing the blinders on people. Many leaders and innovators have been blinded by passion unable to let go before it ruins them. I have found myself blinded by my passion and it cost me the most precious thing in life. And that is the price extremes can take on us. Passion is certainly a great thing, but when it overwhelms, when it blinds, when it rules over you, that is when problems arise.

So yes, a Jedi can feel passion, be passionate. Indeed these are not considered bad things. Yet the essence of the Jedi Path is found in enjoying our passions without letting them rule us, without letting those passion completely direct us. We must be able to temper them with knowledge, with objectivity, with reason. Most find this easy when calm, at peace. When one is serene they are able to see the big picture, to see things without the blinders of passion, to understand the many paths to the main goal, not just the singular path. So Jedi encourage serenity, they know its value. A value in many areas, in many ways.

Yet there is a catch. Serenity often gets tied into Meditation, Enlightenment, on a removal of all of life's distractions. Some find Serenity to be the justification for meditating for five hours in their room. Some denote that you need 3600 hours of meditation to obtain levels of consciousness and fantastic powers. We, as Jedi, do not get the luxury of 35 hours a week of meditation. Jedi do not endorse this, it is not considered a good use of time and life. Serenity is not about hiding away in your bedroom the majority of your life. Being a Jedi serves no one if you are locked away in your room for the majority of your time.

That said - who doesn't need some "me" time. We all need some space, some time to recoup, to recover, to revitalize. There is some many ways to regain our sanity. Some find it in cross-stitch, video games, some in books, some in a nice hot bubble bath, and certainly in meditation. A combination of these, of other things, perhaps cooking, working out, running, the list is as unique and limitless as humanity. We all need some time to simply recharge our batteries and take the world head on fully charged.

What we find in this line is the reminder that we need both. Passion, Serenity, we must not allow one to rule us. We do not want to become some apathetic man on a mountain removed from the dirt of the world serving and helping no one. Likewise we do not want to become so focused and blinded on our passions we miss all the warning signs and/or miss all the roses worth smelling.

That calm center is core to really mastering the first two lines. We have to have that understanding of serenity, of being able to survive the worse of the world and having a sanctuary. Look, there is going to be times life just beats you to the ground. It is going to happen, it has probably happened once or twice or a few times already. It will never stop. Life will be a dominate force applying pressure to your shoulders. You can do everything right and still have some out-of-nowhere event completely rain on the parade. The secret is in knowing your ability to recover, to find things that ease the burden. You are capable of moving forward, of rising again. You may get knocked down, but you are never out of the fight. Thing the glue that holds this together is serenity, a calm center of pure understanding - nothing can destroy your inner peace but you.

Of course the trick is find the inner peace first right? So lets find it. Lets reflect on it.

-= **Day 5 Assignment** =-

Favorite Past-time - Sports? What kind? Football? Playing or watching or both? Video Games? What kinds? FPS, RPG, MMO of said genre? Books? Which genre? Writing, Reading, Both? Music? Creating, Listening, Playing, All of the Above?

You have a day that completely drains you - sanity is gone, you are physically, mentally, emotionally tired. What do you normally do? Has that or do you believe that may change as a Jedi?

Due by Tomorrow.

The Jedi Code - Day Six:
Line Four: Trying to Find a Balance

Yesterday we looked at an element which required finding a balance between extremes. However the line "**there is no chaos; there is harmony**" is truly all about balance. Moderation is all things is a core part of this. Yet like all the lines we have seen, there is a multifaceted element involved. AS we all have experienced, life can be hectic at times, a bit chaotic. Out of nowhere fifty things can pile up on us and we find our time and energy stretched. This line is tackling finding a balance within that, it is about moderation in the things we do, it relates to the previous lines, it is about attuning ourselves to the world around.

A balance in nature and technological advancement. A balance in personal well-being, not neglecting one element over another. It is about tempering our passions and emotional investments with objectivity and reason. As well as tempering our logic with humility and humanity. The beauty of human relationships, whether family or romantic, is the free expression of self and love between one another; a manifestation of feeling. Yet in order to ensure these relationships are not harmful to the self, to our environment, we need to carry that cold hard logic and reason with us.

I have heard it said that this concept can be described as 'moderation in all things.' Interestingly enough that is how most fictional Jedi sources explain and teach the previous line in the Code on Serenity. This concept isn't far off and is a basic and general way to understand what we seeking to stress here. That balance, basically finding harmony within ourselves and with the world around us. There is a goal of moderation. Yes, be healthy, yes eat right, ingest nurturing/beneficial materials - physically, mentally, spiritually, all around seek to gain positive ingredients in life. Yet one should still enjoy, at times, the things that are "bad" for you. Have a piece of cake, enjoy a glass of wine (if of legal age), go bungee jumping (yes, I consider that unhealthy. Okay, I am mostly joking). Ultimately it is a question of what you wish to be an example of.

Like the rest of these subjects we will be tearing into this much more deeply in Tier Two. Harmony has a few facets to the Jedi. All which tie in to the seven main concepts of wellness. Physical, Mental, Emotional, Spiritual, Social, Financial, and Environmental. Harmony is the knot, the bow, the infinity sign, it is what keeps it all tied together. Ensuring that we, as Jedi, do not become so focused in one area that we lose touch with the importance of the others.

My entire Jedi career has been incorporating this one concept. Constantly I found myself out of sync, out of balance, and the results were horrible. Truly one must find an equilibrium within those seven concepts to truly experience the full richness of life. I have had each in their extremes at different points in my life - I can tell you an imbalance is not a proper way to live. You find that balance in your life and you will be truly happy. Now that is of course easier said than done. It took me stages, I had to work through various extremes, and you may have to go through a similar process. Yet the hope here, the goal here, is to help that journey and let you know balance, harmony is in fact possible and simply a wonderful place to be in life (oh and does not stop progress, growth, or discovery, in fact I'd say it only encourages more of it. So no worries stagnation).
Alright enough of my rambling.

-= Day 6 Assignment =-
Guilty Pleasures - Automatically plural. What is it you indulge in and you know you probably shouldn't? Keeping in mind shouldn't is from a certain point of view. But most of us understand an health expert (in any of the seven aforementioned areas) may shake a finger at some of our treats. Still, we know how to spoil ourselves - so what is your preference? Desserts? Champagne Brunch? A day of sports (football, futbol, etc.)and beer with friends? A day of online gaming and junk food? Perhaps

smoking? Your guilty pleasure (remember journals can be viewed by the entire membership - please seek the G rating - if you feel like sharing something that may cross to R or M territory you can PM the administration, the option is there, especially if you have any questions, concerns, or just wish to share this privately regardless of rating.).

Second part of this - Do you feel you have balance in this? Do you have moderation? Or are you sucking down two packs of smoke a day? Are you eating a Double-Quarter Pounder with Cheese everyday for lunch? Drinking a 6 pack of soda a day? Is your guilty pleasure more of a daily exercise, excuse even? Or have you established limits and moderated how much you enjoy your luxuries in life?

Third - If you feel you have moderation, was it always so or did you have to establish limits? How did you determine that? What steps did you take to ensure a more healthy balance? Do you feel you have achieved that balance? Any tips for those seeking to balance the guilty pleasures?

Due Today/ASAP.

THE JEDI CODE - DAY SEVEN:
Line Five: Life and the Force

Ah the Force. The mystical element of the Jedi. The unseen ally, the source of a Jedi's power. In the fiction the Force is described in two ways. One as an energy field created by all living things which flows around and permeates the entire universe. The second is as microscopic organisms which reside in the cells of living beings and has a symbiotic relationship with life. A higher content of these organisms allows better connection, access, and thus ability through the Force.

We have seen real-world comparable ideals. So many Jedi have simply pushed these other theories as the Force. Some Jedi have labeled it Qi (Chi). Some have dubbed it Prana, Mana, Ki, the Holy Spirit, the Tao, Psi, Magickal Ability, God, extention of Gods and/or Goddesses. I have even seen people list it as Gravity, or akin to Einstein's theory of relativity ($E=MC^2$).

Like Jedi Philosophy it is see to find and acknowledge similarities and close our eyes to the differences. Or at least rationalize the differences, excuse them. The Force is a very vague concept delivered through a fictional entertainment medium. It stands to reason that anyone can link it to anything they wanted a make a decent case for it. I am sure if one wanted they could explain how the Force is Water or Air or Gobstoppers; okay the last one may be difficult.

For now - the question is pointless. You, as a Jedi, need not know what the Force is. For the truth is that the Force is Ineffable. The Force is whatever you chose to believe it to be. I leave the mystical to your own belief system. So lets take a new approach to this subject. Let us forego the conjuncture masquerading as Truth about the Force. Instead let us look at the Force as an ideal, just another branch of Jedi Philosophy, one more core aspect to Jedi Ideology.

What is the Force in this context? What is the ideal behind

the Force? Can I sit here and ramble at you for 4 hours straight on this subject? I can, in fact I am confident I could muster 8 hours of rambling on this one subject. But it is definitely better to find your answers rather than be given answers. So let us reflect, let us consider, let us ponder the concept of the Force. Your assignment......

-= Day 7 Assignment =-

"The force is an energy field created by all living things, it surrounds us, it penetrates us, it binds the galaxy together." - A New Hope

"A Jedi's strength flows from the Force." - The Empire Strikes Back

"For my ally is the Force, and a powerful ally it is. Life creates it, makes it grow. Its energy surrounds us and binds us. Luminous beings are we, not this crude matter. You must feel the Force around you; here, between you, me, the tree, the rock, everywhere, yes. Even between the land and the ship." - The Empire Strikes Back

Based upon these quotes - what message do you feel, do you think, is being sent here? What ideological concept(s) can we, as Jedi, take away from this? Overall if one were to look at the Force as merely a ideal for the Jedi, what ideal(s) are being conveyed? **Due ASAP.**

Lesson 2 – Five Goals of the Jedi
General Overview

The Five Goals of the Jedi:
To truly understand what it means to be a Jedi, we need to examine the Jedi Circle. It gives us an understanding of how a Jedi lives. The practices, outlooks, and traits they focus on. Likewise to truly understand the core of Jedi philosophy we need to examine the purpose and motivations behind it. This is accomplished by examining the five goals of the Jedi, which direct purpose to the Jedi philosophy. It is here that we address the question of 'why' a Jedi does what they do.

Originally the goals were taken from the Rules of Behavior as first published by Wizards of the Coast in their Power of the Jedi rulebook for the Star Wars role-playing game. Like many of the core philosophical ideals within the Jedi Path, this was looked at, studied, and debated for validity. Slight changes were made and additions were given to offer a full understanding of what the goals are for a Jedi and following their philosophy.

On their own the Five Goals are very simple to list, but may not be as straight-forward as they seem. Three of these goals did come from a fictional source and thus changes had to be made in how one approaches these ideals. To help understand these goals we will look at them individually. They are listed as a whole as follows:

1.) Train Diligently.
2.) Provide Support.
3.) Render Aid.
4.) Defend Those in Need.
5.) Study of the Force.

On their own they do not provide a lot of structure, since one can accomplish these goals in a variety of ways. But these are generally accompanied by a brief explanation and covered more in-depth within the teachings of the Jedi Philosophy. We will look at each of these elements on their own, offering first the brief explanation often given them, and then looking more closely at what it meant by each of these elements.

Train Diligently:

As usually prudent we will start at the beginning, goal number one, "Train Diligently" which is often accompanied by the following: "*Be capable of fulfilling the role and course of a Jedi.*" When I was training under Mindas Ar'ran in Great Falls, Montana he would say it daily, "train diligently." It was an idea that if you wanted to excel then you needed this. If you wanted it to be second-nature then you must follow this. If you were to be capable of fulfilling the role and ideals of the Jedi then you certainly have to train diligently as a Jedi.

Jedi training covers a wide variety of practices from meditation to physical fitness. They each have a reason for being practiced and they are tied closely to the Jedi ideals. As an example, serenity is tough to accomplish without a basic practice of meditation. This ideal becomes very self-evident within the first week of Jedi training. Thus goal number one, in order to ensure the other four goals listed, we must be capable of fulfilling them.

This is why Jedi spend years training. It is not easy to alter our lifestyle to include more activities. Life gets busy enough without adding in extra work, studies, and practices on top of it. It is essential however that we do, if this is the life we chose to live. Waking up in the morning to meditate and have a light work-out isn't really second-nature to most of us. Thus we have to train ourselves to get into the mindset of better living. Of doing something good for ourselves before we go out and face the world everyday.

Training helps us approach problems and situations as a Jedi. No one is born a Jedi, just as no one is born a Police Officer or President. You can be suited for it, you can excel without trying, but you need to prepare for it, train for it, learn the practices, procedures, and ideals. The best way to excel is to train day-in and day-out. This is why the first goal of any Jedi is to train diligently.

Provide Support:
Listed and explained as "*sometimes the best help, is merely encouragement and support. A Jedi does not always have to be hands-on, but instead provides the needed support.*" Jedi through their training often become pillars of strength, emotionally, spiritually, mentally, and even physically. Because of this many people often turn to the Jedi for support. Whether that is advice on a difficult matter, how best to proceed in a certain situation, discussions on faith, belief, and spirituality, or even just knowing they are capable in moving furniture instead of their 85 year old Grandmother.

People often confuse a Jedi's desire to help others and be of service to mean they volunteer 100% of their time. Or that they should all be members of the Peace Corp. You do not need to look far and wide to find places to help and people who could use a little support. From Community projects to friends in a bad place, there are many places a Jedi can provide their support.

Most of us do this in our lives regardless, Jedi just tend to actively look for the opportunities and chances to act on it. This serves as a reminder that Jedi do not have to be 100% pro-active and go off to every corner of the world to be of service. There are plenty of chances to lend our support right in our own inner-circle. There are many ways for Jedi to be of service in our lives. Whether that is simply a shoulder to cry-on, being the objective adviser on career choice, or picking up some chores around your friend's house because he injured his back. Sometimes it is as simple a few words of encouragement. Just have to look for the chance to offer that support.

Render Aid:
"*Sometimes it is resources that are needed the most. A*

Jedi can give their time, money, services, and/or supplies for the service of others." We are not always in a position to give of ourselves, but when considering of how to be of service to the community and the world we can look at rendering aid. This is meant to remind the Jedi that while we seek to help others and better the world there are many great organizations out there seeking to do just that.

The idea here is that we have a variety of ways to help out. Donating our blood and/or plasma to a local group such as Red Cross. Giving yearly monetary donations to groups like the Salvation Army. Giving our time and helping local organizations such as the Optimist or Rotary clubs, making sure their events have enough people to flourish. Donating food, can goods, and clothing to groups like Goodwill and local homeless shelters.

The Jedi do not need to be a humanitarian organization, they simply need to be willing to help such preexisting groups out and there truly are a plethora of ways to accomplish that. Sometimes a Jedi may live in an area where a natural disaster occurs, here they can also render aid by helping with sand bags, clean-up, search and rescue, and so forth. What we seek to impress here is that a Jedi can find many ways to render aid and help world-betterment, even on a small scale.

Defend Those in Need:
This next goal has the longest explanation because it can be misunderstood. *"Sometimes people need help defending themselves. Whether that is by sticking up for them in a argument or unfair situation. Calling the proper authorities to correct a situation. Or showing that they have someone who will not allow physical harm to come to them. A Jedi defends those in need."*

Defense of others has long been an accepted and understood part of the Jedi Path. Yet due to the way the fiction represents Jedi many take defense of others to be only a physical thing. Fighting in the place of another. Fighting injustice against law-breakers. All these really way-out-there scenarios in which a Jedi must pick up a sword and fight. Which is simply not the case and leads others, even some Jedi, to the wrong conclusions.

Jedi seek to defend those in need, but what is defense? Who is in need? What is the best way to handle the situation? Often times simply a kind word in a heated situation is all that is needed. Some humor injected into a tense situation can change the entire dynamic. Sometimes it is simply standing up for someone getting picked on, whether that is by a friend, family member, boss, co-worker, classmate, and so on. Often times just voicing an opinion can resolve a situation.

This is why diplomacy is a core practice of Jedi. Because they understand that sometimes the best defense is prevention. It is resolution achieved through words. It can be in siding with an individual and letting them know they are not alone. If they seem incapable of standing up for themselves sometimes just having another do so for them can resolve the situation and give the person the courage to stand-up for themselves later on. How one does that is why Jedi study Conflict Resolution so as not to turn a bad situation into a worse one.

However hostile situations can arise and a Jedi may find themselves confronted by a very aggressive and violent individual. This is why physical fitness and self-defense are a part of the Jedi Path and practices as well. Again though, many ways to reach peaceful resolution, so many things are factored into such potential physical confrontations. Jedi are prepared for the worse, but look for the better options. For example, calling the proper authorities always a viable option.

It is a goal of the Jedi to defend those in need, from the planet, to animals, to our fellow humans. Make no mistake, there is a large variety of ways to reach this goal. Many which tie into the two previous goals. Which is a staple of the Jedi Path, this tying with that, that tying in with this, and so forth. This is one of the more tricky goals simply because of the broad scope it entails and the concern over physical confrontation. Hopefully we have conveyed that there are many peaceful ways in fulfilling this goal and those options should always be practiced and sought first. <u>The best Jedi will never be in a physical fight.</u>

Study of the Force:
"A Jedi continues the study and advancement of the Force. Further defining the Force, by continually experiencing, exploring, and understanding it." The Force is a very difficult subject to discuss for two major reasons. The first being that it is mostly ineffable. The second being that it is terminology taken direct from Star Wars which has little to no definitive elements. Even the movies have varied in the explanation of the Force.

For the Jedi the Force is a core concept. Yet it is a fresh concept for us, it is a new element. Most religions, philosophies, and beliefs, have something similar attached to them. A mystical or metaphysical element which they have explored and have formed a general consensus on. The Jedi Community as a whole do not have a singular stance on the Force. Some go with the explanation provided by George Lucas via the character Obi-Wan Kenobi in Star Wars A New Hope, ?an energy field.? Some connect the Force with their already established religion or belief, e.g. they view the Force as the Holy Spirit. Same thing, just a different name. Such as viewing the Force as the Chinese concept of Qi (Chi), simply using a different label.

The reality is the Force is unknown to us and as a whole we have left it open to personal interpretation. Yet we continue, as a whole, to explore the ideas, concepts, and science behind the Force. What is it? Is there abilities and knowledge to be unlocked from it? Where did it come from? How is it connected to life? Is that the same or different than the explanations provided by the fiction?

The one thing we cannot deny is that the Force is core to the Jedi, both fictionally speaking and speaking from an inspirational standpoint. Not to mention that many Jedi feel the Force is key to advancing our studies and path as a whole. We have made leaps and bounds on the philosophical front of our Path since 1998. Now we need to seek to have a better understanding of the more spiritual and mystical element to our Path.

Thus it is a continual goal of the Jedi to advance their understanding, both individually and collectively, of the Force. Our current focus is ensuring that individual understanding, encouraging Jedi to affirm their views, beliefs, and definitions. To solidify their views on such matters. To weigh the variety of views exist and are currently being explored, tested, and studied. Is the Force more biological, perhaps relating to Mitochondria? If so does that take anything away from the more mystical elements and ideals or does that perhaps open a new venue of understanding?

In the end it is a core subject which our scientific knowledge and personal understanding is rather limited. Especially considering paths and beliefs out there which feel they already know the answer to such subjects. So we encourage the continual exploration, advancement, and experience of the Force.

-= Lesson Two Assignment =-

1.) "Use your time. You'll find one day that you have too little of it." - Qui-Gon Jinn. Do you believe this quote to be applicable or simply a nice fictional quote? How do you feel this quote relates to the goals above? Can you apply this 'Jedi thought' to your everyday life?
Due Today.

2.) In which ways do you feel that you personally can accomplish each of these Goals of the Jedi in your everyday life? Really think on it. Something practical you can do in your life to accomplish these goals.
Due in Two Days.

3.) Continue the Five Practices. We will be going back to some of the Intro Lesson Exercises in these areas. Mixing it up a bit. Next week will be completely different set of techniques, so enjoy it while you can.
Incorporating Jedi Practices into Your Life - Daily.
NOTE: These are **not** to replace or be replaced by your current

studies and activities. Meaning, if you already do a specific meditation, you are still to practice what is listed here. If you work-out and cover these exercises you are still to do them at some point. These are supplemental exercises for daily use, to be used in conjunction with your current lifestyle.

- Physical Fitness - Start with some light stretching (touch the toes, reaching for the sky, etc.). A little knee high marching in place. Now - Do 25 Jumping Jacks, 20 Mountain Climbers, 25 Hip Raises, 15 Push-ups, 20 Lunges, 30 Sit-ups, and 30 Squats. Daily, once is fine, any time, I recommend morning right when you get out of bed. Doesn't take me more than 10 minutes to complete; counting off days.
- Meditation - Going back to the Breath. I want you to just breathe. This will be your meditation for now. Just take a moment from time to time and just close your eyes and breathe deeply for a few moments. When in the shower, when waiting for something to load, in the morning before starting the morning routine, before bed, etc. Just take a moment and breathe.
- Awareness - Take a moment and just take in your surroundings. Above you, behind you, to the sides, below, just look around, note the things you see. To the left a wall with pictures, a smoke detector above me, window in front, beige house across the street. Do this when out for a walk, when you walk into a new room, go to the movies, etc. Do not try to catalog everything, do not take twenty minutes in the doorway looking at everything, just take the moment and note what you can. The things and people around you.
- Diplomacy - This one we are just going to focus more on listening to others. What is being said, the words used. How is it being said, the tone used. And not reacting either way to the words or tone, but instead focusing on meaning, the purpose. "Take out the dang garbage!" "Sure

thing." Stop what you are doing, get it done. After a little time with that, you can start requesting a please. Seek to remove the emotion, and simply focus on what is truly being said and/or asked. And then act accordingly.
•Self-Discipline - This should be obvious. Just actually follow through on these practices daily. Incorporate them and keep them up for as long as you are in this program.

How to Perform the Exercises Listed:

Jumping Jacks: Feet together, arms at your sides, jump spreading your feet shoulder width apart and bring your arms above your head all in one motion.

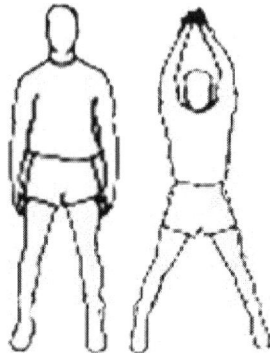

Mountain Climbers: Get into the starting Push-up Position. Now, you push off with your leg, bring the knee into the chest, while the other leg stays extended. Kick your leg back and bring the other knee into the chest.

Hip Raise: Lay with your back flat on the ground with knees bent - as if doing sit-ups. Now simply raise your hips off the ground while keeping your shoulders on the ground. Creating a straight diagonal line from knees to shoulders.

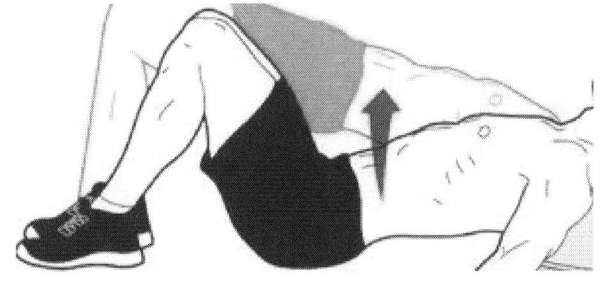

Push-ups: Position yourself face down on the floor, balancing on your toes/knees and hands. Your hands should be wider than shoulders, body in a straight line from head to toe. Don't sag in the middle and don't stick your butt up in the air. Slowly bend your arms and lower your body to the floor, stopping when your elbows are at 90 degrees. Exhale and push back up.

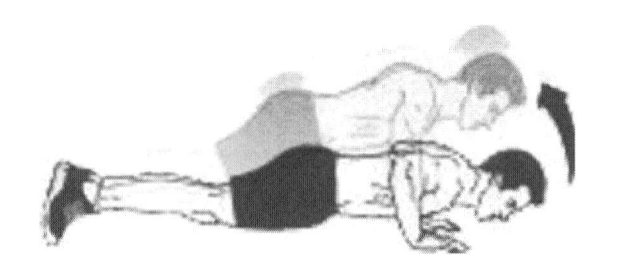

Lunges: Stand, comfortably, extend one leg forward, bending at the knee. Do <u>Not </u>let your other knee hit the ground. Stand back up, alternate legs.

Sit-ups: Lie down on the floor on your back and bend your knees, placing your hands behind your head or across your chest. Pull your belly button towards your spine, and flatten your lower back against the floor. Slowly contract your abdominal muscles, bringing your shoulder blades about one or two inches off the floor. Exhale as you come up and keep your neck straight, chin up. Hold at the top of the movement for a few seconds, breathing continuously. Slowly lower back down, but don't relax all the way.

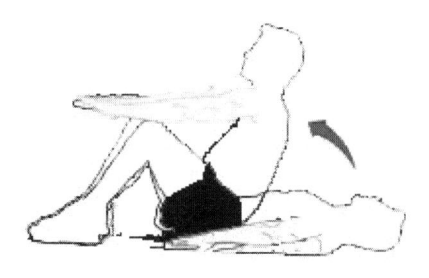

Squats: Stand with feet hip-width apart, toes facing straight ahead or angled slightly outward. Slowly bend the knees and lower hips towards the floor, keeping your torso straight and abs pulled in tight. Keep your knees behind your toes; make sure everything's pointing in the same direction. Do not go lower than 90 degrees.

Five Goals - Day Three:
Application

The Jedi Way is found in living. One cannot be a Jedi by hiding from life. As much as we would often like to simply disappear to some Temple in the middle of nowhere this is hardly living as a Jedi. The fictional Jedi were not removed from the hustle and bustle of everyday life. Their main staging grounds were at the heart of civilization. They were traveling among average citizens and they continually were sent out to help deal with major issues. This is a far different concept than something like the Shaolin Temple.

We are not meant to be some mysterious and cloistered order which practices in our forest spouting platitudes of enlightenment (just be clear, this is not a shot or commentary about Shaolin). Jedi are everyday people who recognize the need of more kindness, more support, more help, more light, if you will, in the world. They recognize that the world can be chaotic, it can seem heavy, dark, and hopeless. Yet this is not fully the case and even still the more obstacles we are presented the better we get at overcoming them.

In the end, it is the feeling of the Jedi that we can be of use, of benefit, of positive enforcement in our everyday lives. That how we live, what we live by, what we do with our lives means something. It does have an effect, if only a small one. But a small positive change, a bright example of humanity is so much better than none. It is not about changing how the world works. Rather it is about changing how we work with the world.

We each of the power to make an impact in other people's lives. We may not even be aware of it. We may simply be the example of how to live to some unspoken observer. Who takes our lead, they follow the ideals, the concepts presented by our everyday actions. What you say, how you say it, what you do, how you do it, all of this matters.

This is the ideal, the concept behind the Five Goals of the Jedi. That your actions, how you live, the purpose you place upon your life does affect the world; it certainly affects your own world, your own circle of friends and family. Be the guide, be the lighthouse that helps others find their way through the chaotic waters of life. The goals of the Jedi help guide one in this endeavor.

I'll be discussing application of the goals next. Some of this should recap what was previously said. It is core we explore how we can live by these and be examples of them. For the past two days you had a chance to think of ways to incorporate these into your life. Now we can explore that a bit more together. See if we get some overlap.

First we must be capable. We must be able to handle us a task. To guide and live our own lives in a positive and beneficial manner. So we study, we train, practice, exercise, live by the ideals of our path. Thus we denote Train Diligently. This application in everyday life is simple - because you should be doing it daily. Yes, even those small daily practices given to you each week enforce and highlight this principle.

How can we provide support? So many ways. By supporting a friend's decision. By being a shoulder to cry on and reminding them how strong and capable they truly are. By seeing the good, the positive, the beneficial in those around us and reminding them of their value. We want to enforce their foundation, remind them they are good, with or without anyone. We can support them by helping in endeavors, by picking chores when they are bogged down.

Spouse is buried with work - so you pick-up their chores until things mellow out. Give them some time to rest and regain themselves. This works with friends, school, it is simply about temporarily picking up some of the burden and supporting a person through a tough time. While letting them have self-reliance and gaining from the experience which life has given. You can support your community with liter pick-up, park clean-ups, and so forth. Truly the only limitation is your own desire and imagination.

Render Aid is an easy application. Lets rephrase it - Community Service. This can be donating money, clothes, can goods, toys, blood, et cetera. This can be volunteering at any number of service projects. Teaching to Read, helping homeless families find a job and housing, working at an animal shelter. Truly many organizations and causes out there to get involved in. I like projects which seek to treat/eliminate problems rather than simply throwing a band-aid on them - like putting schools and water purifying devices in Africa rather than simply giving clean water. Personal preference, obviously both render aid. So many ways to render aid.

We do not always have the time or money to fulfill this area. But seek to combine it. Support, Aid, Jedi Ideals, and Your own Fun - example I ran a Spartan Race and personally raised money for a good organization (on top of the race itself donating to a good cause). This one thing had a direct and beneficial impact on many areas of the Jedi Path. So you can certainly find a way to accomplish many things at once without burying yourself.

Application of defending those in need can be foggy. Most people automatically start getting visions of lightsabers dancing in their head. It is not about combat. Can it be? It could, in the worse case scenario violence could be what is hinted at here. But there are many ways to defend those in need. Helping at an Animal Shelter is in fact one. Animals are in need, they require protection. And that just means food, water, and shelter, perhaps funding and work at a shelter to keep it going.

It could be showing verbal support for a person being picked on or bullied. Letting them know they are not alone, that they do not have to accept that as life, and that you can defend their character, their life. It can mean defending an innocent person from prosecution. It can be defending one's religious freedom, sexual freedom, really. The Earth is in need of defense is it not? Environmental Protection groups (decent, legitimate ones) can be a place to put your defending muscles to work. Endangered Species. Truly there are a lot of things in this world that could use a champion. Defend those in love, those chasing a dream, those fighting everyday simply to see the people the love smile. None of this demands physical or violent defense. One last application of defense - calling the proper authorities. Remove the bad element, not simply push it onto someone else. Don't play hero, instead be a hero by getting the right people involved to ensure a difference is made.

Application of Studying the Force is simple observation and reflection. It is a very personal subject. And one I cannot give you answers on. The Force is Ineffable - it is left for you to explore, experience, and thus define. You must find your answers through open, honest, and sincere study. Let your exploration, your experience, guide you while you seek the objective, calm, and focused mind which will provide the best answers. Boldly explore new concepts and ideas and find your answers. Meditation, Prayer, following the other Goals, do not ignore the concept of the Force. Develop it.

In the future this will no doubt become critical information which will help us find similarities in our diverse field. The Jedi Path is very young, we are just beginning. As we grow and explore individually, the more pieces of puzzle we gain and obtain. In this we will be in a much better position in the future to offer more core ideals on this ineffable force which we hold to be invaluable to living as a Jedi. So study, explore, experience, and find your own definition, then be willing to share and discuss with other Jedi. So we may all learn from one another and use our diversity as a strong tool in progress.

-= Lesson 2 Day 3 Assignment =-

"*Anyone can handle a weapon. Reason is much more difficult to wield. Remember that the next time you?re tempted to settle an argument with a lightsaber.*" - Luminara Unduli
"*Suspend your judgment, and every being has something to teach you.*" - Qui-Gon Jinn
"*Selflessness is the only antidote to evil. It provides the light that destroys the dark.*" - Corran Horn

Which quote do you feel is applicable to the lesson? All? None? Why or Why not? You have a favorite in this group? What do the quotes say or how do they enforce concepts above, if at all?
Due in Two Days.

Five Goals - Day Four:
History

     The main meat of the Goals of the Jedi come from the Jedi Rules of Behavior. Which in turn come from the Power of the Jedi source book (my copy being published and picked up in 2002). The other two elements of the Rules were fleshed out by myself and my roommate at the time Mindas Ar'ran. He was the guy I bounced my ideas off of since he had a detached view (didn't call or consider himself a Jedi), experience in the Jedi Community, and a pretty knowledgeable individual. Anyhow the meat being Provide Support, Render Aid, and Defend the Weak. The additions being Train Diligently and Study the Force.

     There isn't much history to be shared here. I have never seen these elements taught anywhere else. Not in this fashion. there always seems to be some sort of vague concept of helping others, but I have ever seen it defined in a day-to-day process. Or how it actually relates to living as a Jedi. Personally I find it a simple concept. Jedi understand all life is connected (in one form or another), they understand the importance of the whole, and that each unique piece is required to finish the mosaic. Thus there is a desire to grow beyond ourselves, to improve ourselves so that we may improve the quality of life of those around us, those we meet, and the world in general. Jedi tend to understand that if you continually let things go because you are expecting someone else to do them, they will never get done. If you want to see change in this world, you must affect the change, even be the catalyst of that change.

     I am pseudo-historian. I play at it. I enjoy history, but I am really a horrible historian. A horrible record-keeper in general; which no good at keeping records, no good at being a historian. So it is something I admire and try my hand at simply because there is one other person out there trying to preserve our history.

     So I find these types of lessons important. I enjoy writing

them. I enjoy sharing how concepts developed, what our first lessons on the subject looked like, what processes we went through to get to where we are. I do not want you to think that I magically developed these lessons first try. Or this is how our community has always been (or certainly that all Jedi sites are the same). There has been a lot of trial and error over the years. And I personally believe it is important to acknowledge the growth and evolution of our path. It is my hope that it will encourage you, or at least show you, that things are always being improved upon, nothing is final, and you can build/develop your own lessons built upon the foundations (or ruins) of previous ones.

    The first lesson I can find on the Five Goals of the Jedi was written in 2006 at the Jedi Organization (formerly known as JEDI). At this time I had taken over as the Administrator of the site and was putting into affect my vision for the Jedi Community. If you remember the previous history lesson - that didn't work out per se, but eventually lead to the creation of the JAO upon those ashes (with much thanks owed to an over-zealous student named Jasta Gar'su).

    Anyhow, I figured I'd share that first lesson with you. A bit of history. Fair warning. I am keeping in all the horrible typing errors (some just bonehead spelling mistakes). I do this again to show the growth in the lessons. An understanding that presentation is important. I also want to show my own growth. No one starts out perfect and regardless of experience or age, you can always grow and better yourself. So as embarrassing as it is for me, I have kept the original lesson intact.

Five Goals of the Jedi - Written by Opie Macleod - Nov. 6, 2006 8:44 PM

Quote

Five Goals of the Jedi:
1- Train Dillegently: Be capable of fulfilling the goals and course of the Jedi.
2- Provide Support: A Jedi does not always serve directly. We must take a backseat at times and provide support for those

frontrunners.
3- Render Aid: A Jedi is not always needed physically. Sometimes what is needed is our time, caring, and/or supplies.
4- Defend the Weak: Whether by getting extra help or stepping in physically, a Jedi must defend those in need.
5- Study the Force: Continue to Experience, Explore, and Understand the Force.

Understanding and putting the Goals into Practice:
1- Train Dillegently:
As humans we will come across various situations in life. Car accidents to angry costumers, to our own family problems. There are many things that can derail our lives, as Jedi we train to handle these unexpected situations. Steadying and keeping a calm observant mind. A fit and capable body. Awareness to use diplomacy in event he most stressful situations.

When helping out other non-profit groups, it is vital to be preapred and capable to handle all situations that may arise. From helping with a minor dispute, to recalling a person's face and clothes who stole someone's purse at an event.

2- Provide Support:
It is a major misconception that as Jedi we have to "save the world." In this idea many wonder about our purpose since there are many great groups already helping out around the world (Red Cross, Peace Corps, etc). But a key part of being a Jedi is supporting others in their own causes.

Support varies from group to group, from individual to individual.. Sometimes support is a a Friendly Smile and open ear, sometimes support is encouragement and not allowing another person to give-up. Other times it can be a weekend investment in a fundraiser. As Jedi we need to be able and willing to provide support to the varius people who request/need it.

3- Render Aid:
Things happen in life that are not pleasant. We have natural and human disaters alike and it is in these times that Aid is required. As Jedi we must step up and provide what Aid we can at any given moment. Whether you are front lines building sandbag barriers, or answering phones to take people's donations, or donating yourself.. Aid comes in many forms.

In times of need a Jedi has to render proper aid. But we all have different talents and areas in which we excel in and can give more freely. There is always a area in which one can be of service.

4- Defend the Weak:
Most people apply this to Humans. Defending weaker humans, and fromt hat people think of getting into fights or having to step inbetween fights. But that is not the only thing a Jedi must be aware of. Weak is to reference anything that cannot properly defend itself.

Jedi respects life, in all forms. All things are connected and Jedi feel that connection. SO they seek to help others in need. In this Jedi defend the Weak, meaning they protect those who cannot. This can be a Bug on the sidewalk, choosing to not step on it, making sure someone else does not step on it. A starving man, Teach that man to fish, as the proverb goes.

A Jedi does not just solve people's problems or take those problems upon themselves. A Jedi must Defend others by helping them defend themselves. A Jedi does not just fight someone's battles, but advises them on proper course of action, on how to stand-up and defend themselves, direct them to others who can teach them skills necessary for surviving life. In this a Jedi defends weaker lfie by strengthing it, helping it grow.

5- Study the Force:
As mention a Jedi feels a conenction to all life and how all life is

connected. This Connection is the Force, and learning more about the Force is a key part of being a Jedi. There are many Paths out there that have undertaken the huge task of studying the mystery of life, of energy. And the Jedi is the youngest out there, but that doesn't mean we are least knowledgable.

A Jedi does not discount other Paths and their previous reseach in the field of the ineffable. But a Jedi is not bound by other Paths and their previous research either. We are free to research all relevant fields and make our own discoveries and methodologies in the Force.

It is key for the Jedi to explore, experience, and define the Force on their own terms. Not bogged down by what has already been said, but finding what works best for us. We may be re-inventing the wheel, but it is something that we as a Path must embark on.

Hopefully this small glimpse helps in this weeks lesson and understanding. A lot of the times, when we look back we don't see a lot of change. What we notice is small things being worked on. I feel this speaks to the value of the main concept. The core concept is sound, it is simply our understanding and delivery that grows and changes. If nothing else, it has been a light week, with a constant drilling of concepts. So no excuse not to remember these and the ideas behind them from this point forward.

-= Lesson 2 Day 4 Assignment =-

Personal Update Time. How are things going? With the practices? With life? How is the Jedi Path working for you? Easy integrating it into your daily routine? Just checking in with you - how is it going?

FIVE GOALS - DAY SIX:
Living It

    One of the things I look to stress with the Jedi Path is living it. Over the past couple of weeks I am sure that has been a core message. If not, I really need to work on my presentation skills. In any case, as Jedi we cannot hide in a corner all our lives. We have chosen a path that demands we involve ourselves in our life. No taking a backseat to life, but jumping in and taking control of the wheel of life.

    Each us of are strong and capable individuals who are seeking to grow and solidify that personal strength. We want to accomplish more than just being an observer to life. You are the main player, the main actor in the story of your life, yet you can also be a strong supporting role in the lives of many others. Making an impact in other people's lives for the better. Spreading positive and beneficial concepts, examples, and actions throughout the world.

    The Goals of the Jedi remind us that the Jedi Path is a multifaceted lifestyle. There is a core focus on the self, on being the best of who we can be. Of living in a way that best speaks to us and makes us feel good on the inside. Something when we look in the mirror we can smile and take pride in. Yet, there are three other goals that remind us that being a Jedi is not solely found within. It must be lived, it must be experienced, it must be shared through our actions. We must get out there and DO, LIVE, SHARE. We recognize the best way for that to have a positive and beneficial affect for everyone is to be capable, prepared, and ready to embrace that role. Thus we train.

    In the end we are reminded that being a Jedi starts within and flows outwardly. The reason you are called a Jedi from day one, is because from day one life is going to through things at you. Life doesn't wait for you to be an experienced, skilled, and fully trained Jedi. Thus the opportunities to live as a Jedi tend to show up right away. You do not have all the tools in your Jedi Toolbox yet, but you do have enough to focus your actions and reactions appropriately.

This week we have been looking at ways to apply the goals of the Jedi in a practical way in our everyday lives. Nothing fancy. No traveling to the Congo to ensure implementation of continual fresh water resources (at least not yet). Certainly though we have acknowledged that even a smile to a passerby on the street is a form of passing on a positive and beneficial outlook. Small to large, we acknowledge that we are not passengers, we are in control, we have the power to make a difference, we have the ability to affect change, we are capable of shaping our lives in whatever manner we chose. The real question we face is - What will we chose? Fortunately, as Jedi, we get a lot of directions, a lot of signs helping to point us at various ways we can go.

-= Lesson 2 Day 6 Assignment =-

I find it a good practice to keep a reminder of things we have gratitude for. This helps in sharing the positive outlook and keeping our focus. So, what are you thankful for? What things do you have gratitude for?
Due by Tomorrow.

Lesson Three - Five Traits of the Jedi:
Overview.

In the Jedi Circle there are five traits listed for the Jedi. Patience, Objectivity, Reliability, Humility, and Wisdom. We will be looking at these and briefly covering the application of these traits in our daily lives as Jedi. Rest assured this is not the last time you will see these elements. As mentioned in the Introduction Lesson every aspect of the Jedi Circle gets a full two weeks to itself. The reason being full application, full experience, full understanding.

I do not expect you to get this perfect on day one. This is a process. It is why we have tiers of training. Why Jedi are at different levels of experience and understanding. It does take time to fully live and apply these concepts to your life. Especially if they are the thing furthest from what you are use to doing. Habits are hard to break and it is hard to form new ones.

Still it is important for you to gain understanding on why we do what we do. What is expected of you as a Jedi and what elements really factor into living as a Jedi in our everyday life. Now you may not perfect this over the course of the week, but it gives you that head start for when the next level of training begins. Everyday seek to incorporate Patience, Objectivity, Reliability, Humility, and Wisdom into your life.

Now what does that mean? How do we, as Jedi, do that exactly? For the next week we will be covering each topic individually. Which means a bit more checking in on your part than previous lessons. But lets have a brief look at them right now so we can begin the journey of embodying these elements.

Patience. Oh patience. That is a tough one. Not something one can truly teach. It has to be learned, exercised. It is something that comes from acting patient when you are feeling anything but. It is repetition. No worries, I wouldn't leave you without some ideas on how to cultivate patience. First thing is to use the reliable old pragmatic approach. Ask yourself - what does it matter? Is it worth it? What is being solved by being impatient? Impatience rarely, if ever, works in our favor. In fact it generally when rushed when we forget things, we miss tiny, but important details, we do things we wouldn't normally do. All because we feel hurried and have a -must accomplish Now- mentality.

So step one - Slow down, breathe, then think! What good is this? Does being fifteen minutes late differ from ten minutes? Step two - Remember that most accidents and things left behind happen when rushed. So stop, take the extra two minutes to run through your head and double-check what you need. Bring it down a notch. Remember that you are in control of you. You get to say whether or not you are rushed.

Step three- Minimize your time via organization. Have a big meeting or report due tomorrow? Get everything in order the night before. Lay out your clothes. Get your materials all together, everything from keys, wallet, to report, and pens.

Patience - for a Jedi it is time to eat as well. We all have things we feel the need to accomplish and get done. But rushing off isn't the answer and rarely changes things in our favor. So be patient with yourself, with your training, with your life. Tackle issues as they arise and remember that you have time. Sure, make the most of that time, but do not miss the beauty of it due to impatience.

Objectivity. Probably one of the most important aspects of being a Jedi. Objectivity, Fairness, the ability and desire to seek the truth, to seek knowledge, to find the whole story. Objectivity is a bit tough because we are naturally bias in certain ways. Family, Friends, Passions, these automatically place a certain bias and color our lens. Our experiences do the same. Have enough bad experiences at an Amusement Park and you won't have a fair outlook towards them.

This, my friends, is step one in Objectivity. Recognizing our own bias. In this we can fully admit when we have a biased view and thus begin to look around it. Example: I really dislike baseball. I think it is a boring and horrible sport. Yet I have bad experiences with Baseball, from little league, to going to baseball games, my experiences have colored my perception of baseball. Yet, because I am aware of this, I can begin to look past it. I can listen openly and fairly to people who enjoy baseball. From them I can understand and even see the value and other side of baseball which I have not and do not experience. In this I can defend baseball to those who may have a view such as myself. I can help share the knowledge I gained so they may understand that just because we have this view, just because we had these experiences, does not mean that is fact. It is simply our view, our opinion, based upon our own experiences.

    This is a core part of objectivity, being able to look beyond your own personal bias and find the truth of the whole. It is about getting that bird's eye view instead of just sticking to our tunnel vision view of life. It is about not accepting broad labels, but understanding that there is a different side to every story. That there are exceptions to the rule. That there is truth and beauty to be found everywhere.

    Do not allow yourself to be pigeon-holed, blinded, or made to see with blinders on. Take in the whole, understand every side, seek knowledge, seek understanding. Be fair and objective in all things. Yourself, your life, all that you do. Be fair, be objective.

    Reliability. I can keep this much shorter than the others. It is simple. Be reliable. How? Do not promise more than you can keep. Or another way to look at it, promise little, deliver much. Your word is your bond, it is something that should be considered golden. More valuable than any currency. When you say you are going to be somewhere - You Be There. If unsure, do not say you will. Be open, be honest, say what you mean.

    I said I'd release Tier One by January 2013 at the time of writing, we aren't there yet. But I am already getting prepared to move over lessons. And start the process of changing the format and we are over a month away. Promise made - promise delivered. Be reliable. If not before - that changes now.

    Humility. Simply put - Don't brag. Joke, sure, but do not go around boosting about who you are and what you can do. If there is an actual need and it fits into the situation, okay, but truly, how often is that going to happen? Simple here as well, talk softly and carrying a big stick. Big talk is just that - talk. Let your deeds speak for you.

This is the core of this element. Deeds, Actions. Some people will brag about having three black belts and how they are a master this and master that. Yet all their actions, even online, scream otherwise. Talk is cheap. It is in the doing that we find true worth.

this lies into what we were saying above. Say little, deliver much. Don't go around saying you are going to do this and you are going to do that. Instead, focus, buckle down, and get it done. Shock, surprise, amaze people with what you do - not what you say.

Wisdom. Best way to understand this element is simply to understand that Knowledge + Experience = Wisdom. It is not just in knowing, it is in doing, in applying, in gaining experience that we find our wisdom. Jedi do not discount knowledge, they seek, they yearn for it. But it doesn't stop there, what good is knowledge if it is not applied? Thus Jedi experience, they test, they try, and they take that knowledge and experience it. With experience, with time, with study we find wisdom comes as the by-product.

Wisdom isn't repeated. You cannot quote 365 zen and expected to be considered wise. That is not wisdom. That is knowledge. That is knowing and memorizing something. But where is the application? Where is the personal experience? Where is the know-how? Many will shove books down your throat and tell you to learn it. May work in school, but for the Jedi it is non-sense.

Our wisdom is found in living as Jedi. In doing. No one where is going to force a book, lesson, or concept on you that they don't have five different experiences with. This is relevant to the way - here is a personal example. That is core. Wisdom is found in application, in taking our knowledge and living it every single day. Through ups, through downs, through successes, through failures. And so yes, there have been and there will be failures and you best believe there is core wisdom to be found within them.

    Overall: Patience - Objectivity - Reliability - Humility - Wisdom. Learn it, Know it, Live it. Core Traits of being a Jedi.

-= Lesson Three Assignment One =-

Incorporating Jedi Practices into Your Life - Daily. Part Four: NOTE: These are not to replace or be replaced by your current studies and activities. Meaning, if you already do a specific meditation, you are still to practice what is listed here. If you work-out and cover these exercises you are still to do them at some point. These are supplemental exercises for daily use, to be used in conjunction with your current lifestyle.

- **Physical Fitness** - Start with some light stretching (touch the toes, reaching for the sky, etc.). A little knee high marching in place. Now - Do 25 Jumping Jacks, 12 Knee Raise Push-ups, 30 Sprinter Sit-ups, 20 Chair Dips, and 30 Squat Reaches (with light weights if able). Daily, Once, any time; I recommend morning right when you get out of bed. Doesn't take me more than 10 minutes to complete (five minutes is my average time). Pictures At the End. As a side-note, you can rest, mid-set break, but I prefer one shot and just make sure you accomplish the numbers given.

- **Meditation** - Way back in a time long forgotten the Jedi adapted a technique for their use. Okay so it was 1999 and the popular Meditation for Jedi at the time was called the Calming Breath. It was a basic breathing exercise done in Yoga practice. Basic Breath Counting. This will be your week long Meditation Practice - at least once a day, twice preferred, and any time you can fit it beyond those times

in works good too. Main goal is to be able to do Step 4 anytime during the day. Helps when feeling stressed or rushed.
Technique Listed after the Physical Exercises.

- **Awareness** - Emotional Awareness Time. Previously we had a how does that make you feel exercise This is basically the same, but more focus on your own emotional responses to outside stimuli. I want you to be completely aware of how things make you feel and how those feelings can illicit reaction without us fully being aware of it. No more, we will catch it and gain awareness over it. So - Mindfulness on Emotional Awareness. i recommend a small notepad you can jot things down in. Or you can use your cellphone, as most have a memo or notepad feature these days. Either way, I want you to track your emotional responses. What ticks you off? What wears your patience? What makes you laugh? Happy, mad, sad, jealous, frustrated, giddy, absent-minded? Seek, find, record. Be aware of the plethora of emotions you feel in a day. Understand it, seek the triggers.

- **Diplomacy** - We have covered tone, ours, others, we have noted the difference it makes in our interactions. How it plays a part in what we do and how we do something. Now we will look at middle ground. Compromise. Now many of us do not get a chance to practice this often, yet it may be more prevalent than one might think. Conflict on what to have for dinner, when to take out the garbage, requested a favor from, et cetera. So be mindful, there may be more examples on this closer than you think. And this offers you the chance to explore finding the middle ground via different mediums as well.
Things to consider - If two people are arguing, what is the middle ground, how could a fair settlement be reached? What information is lacking? If asked to do something

you do not wish to do - is there a middle-ground? A compromise to be had? Seek fair and equatable terms, middle-ground means sacrifice on your part as well. Friend asks to borrow money for lunch, but you only have enough for you, what is the middle-ground?
Places to Consider - If you find your life is not providing any place to really look, judge, and practice this, take it to world. TV, Radio, Movies, Books, Video Games, Strangers at a coffee shop. Simply consider the situation and work through the process. What does both parties want? They obviously can't agree, so what would be a fair compromise to the situation? How do we get a win/win out of this conflict?

- **Self-Discipline** - This should be clockwork by now. Just actually follow through on these practices daily. Incorporate them and keep them up for as long as you are in this program. Hey something that didn't change. Congrats! Now - Go Live as a Jedi. Apply apply apply - not just learning, not just knowing, DO! Is it sinking in yet?

Today's Assignment:

Example Time - Give a personal example of when your patience was tested and you remained patient. Give a personal example of when you were bias, but sought the other side of the story, displaying objectivity and fairness. Personal example of when you were counted on and were proven reliable. Personal example of humility. And last but not least personal example of exercising wisdom.

If you cannot think of one for a Element, that is fine. Simply say as such. A heads-up, we will be revisiting this at the end of the week and I will be expecting brand new examples from over the course of this week. So keep that in mind. Remember it is all about living it.

Due Today.

-=-

How to Perform the Exercises Listed:
Jumping Jacks:
Feet together, arms at your sides, jump spreading your feet shoulder width apart and bring your arms above your head all in one motion.

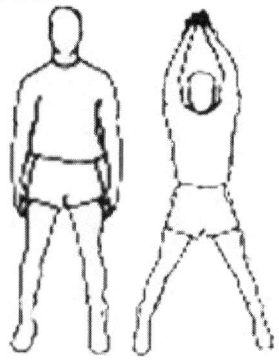

Push-ups with Knee Raise:
Normal Push-up except when the up position bring your knee to your chest. Alternate legs. So one push-up, right knee. Down, up, left knee, down, up, right knee, et cetera.

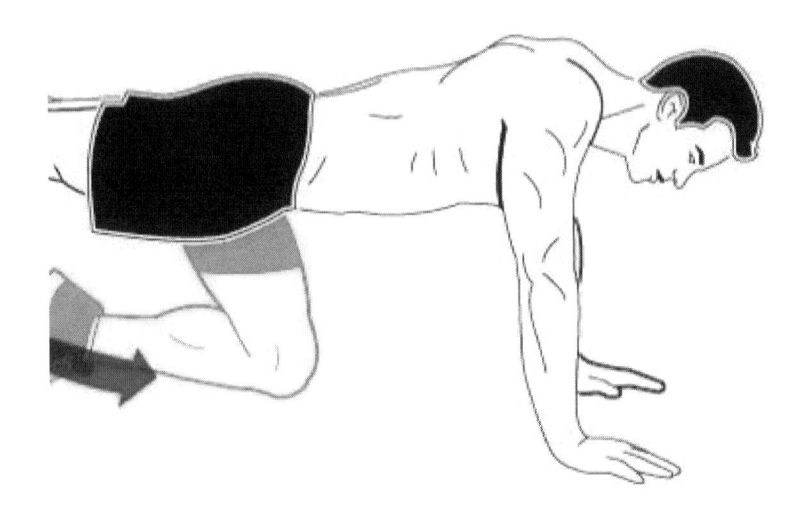

Sprinter Sit-ups:
Lay flat on the ground, legs stretched out. Sit-up, as you do bring your knee into your chest, arms like you are running. Lay back down. Alternate legs, similar to the push-ups.

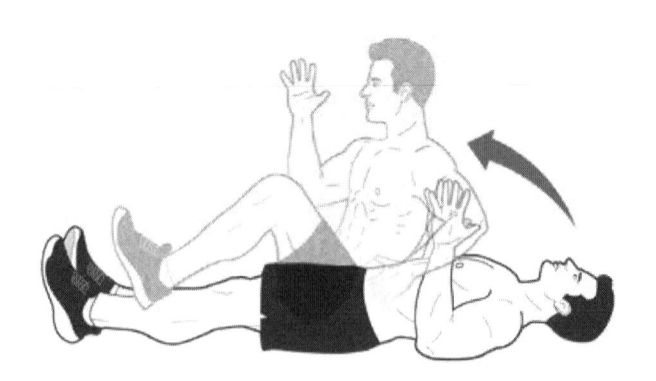

Chair Dips:
Using a chair or bench, support yourself up with your arms straight, back to the chair, butt parallel to the seat. Lower yourself down, bending at the elbows. Your back should not touch the chair, but should be close to it. You don't want to be too far out. Straighten your arms to raise yourself back up.

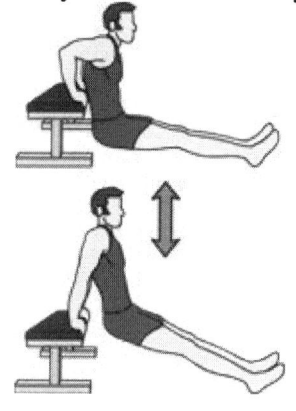

Weighted Squat Reaches:
Normal Squats, but when you come up reach your hands to the sky. If you have 2 or 3 lbs. weights, feel free to use them.

Calming Breath:
Quote

Preparation:
Wear loose fitting attire, so that you are comfortable. Make sure that you can breathe through your nose. If you have a cold, do not practice this exercise until you can breathe clearly.

Step One:
Lie flat on your back. Put one hand on your stomach and the other hand on your chest. Relax.
Inhale so that the hand on your stomach rises, while the hand on your chest is still. Exhale so that the hand on your stomach goes down again, and the hand on your chest remains still. Repeat for 5 breaths.
Now, when you inhale, breathe in so that the hand on your chest rises, while the hand on your stomach is still. Exhale so that the

hand on your chest goes down again, while the hand on your stomach remains still. Repeat for 5 breaths.
Alternate between stomach and chest breathing for 5 minutes. Make sure you've mastered this step before moving on.

Step Two:
This step combines stomach and chest breathing into one breath. This is the Calming Breath.
Lie flat on your back. Put one hand on your stomach and the other hand on your chest. Relax.
Begin by stomach breathing. When you feel you can't inhale any more in this manner, switch to chest breathing, until the upper parts of your lungs are filled. Then exhale by chest breathing first, progressing to stomach breathing so that you empty the lungs fully. Repeat for 5 minutes.
Breathe slowly. If you feel dizzy, slow down, you are breathing too fast. If you are out of breath, you are breathing too slowly. Listen to your own body's messages. If you are having difficulty distinguishing chest breathing from stomach breathing, go back to Step One.

Step Three:
Stand or sit with your back straight.
Use the Calming Breath and follow this pattern. You will have to count the rhythm in your head. I will teach you the rhythm 4-4-4. Count to 4 while inhaling; hold your breath and count to 4 then count to 4 while exhaling. Once you've mastered this you may use a 4-4-4-4 rhythm is you prefer. It adds and extra step of holding your breath after exhaling and counting to 4. Take care not to hold your breath too long. Again, listen to your body. Repeat for 5 minutes, or until you are calm.
Practice so that the Calming Breath becomes effortless, and inaudible. You should breathe no louder than usual. Once you have mastered the technique, it should be invisible to the untrained eye, <u>making it useful in almost any situation.</u>

The Five Traits - Day Two:
Patience

There is no bigger tool to the Jedi than patience. Patience serves a Jedi very well in all manner of practices and situations. First as Jedi we need to understand that nothing is going to come to us over night. We will not wake-up one morning and find out we are Jedi Masters, not without plenty of time and training of course. Thus patience proves us the ability to see our training through the rest of our lives.

Patience also applies to just about every trait one can associate with the Jedi. When we think of diplomacy, emotional control, self-discipline, peace, serenity, learning, teaching, et cetera we can see the value of patience within these things. Each one will require a Jedi to be patient and to exercise that patience more than once.

I am sure we can all recall a moment, a few moments, in our lives where patience would have served us best. We can find ourselves rushing around, in a hurry due to various events in life. Yet in rushing around, when in a hurry this is when it is most important to slow down. To stop and consider what we may forget. Ever had a moment when you were rushing around to get to work, and appointment, or school, and because you were rushing you forgot something vitally important? It is in these times that we have to stop and get back into our normal speed.

Sure, we may be late by doing this. But by rushing we can create bigger problems and make ourselves more late and worse. An example of this can be seen in someone who is rushing home from an appointment to get changed and make it into work on time. They inconvenience two other people to cover for them so they can make the appointment and get to work on time. In rushing home they are speeding and as a result get into a car accident. 2 hours later they make it home, it could have been worse. And it could have been avoided in more ways than one.

Patience would have served very well.

When things are at their busiest, most chaotic, that is when we must be at our most patient. This does not mean moving like turtle or not acting at all. It seems means we must exercise patience and understanding. Patience with ourselves, with others, with mistakes, with the unexpected. You can still be acting, reacting, moving a mile a minute and still using your patience within the situation and the people around you.

The idea of patience is not to get flustered, not to get overwhelmed, and not to lose track of the important details within the moment. To remain centered, calm, and focused on the situation at hand. To handle things logically, in order, as they come. While a ton of bricks may drop on you, may tackling them logically, in a methodical order you can handle each brick one by one in a very fast and efficient manner. As the saying goes, ?more speed, less haste.?

Patience can seem hard to develop, falls under the same issue as Self-discipline. It is not truly something that can be taught our passed on, merely something explained and practiced daily. This presents a challenge to Jedi Hopefuls, as they are in complete control of themselves and their training. Will you seek to develop patience daily? Or will you simply allow yourself excuses and rationalize your inaction?

To help develop patience one should seek not only to practice it daily, but to consciously practice it daily. You may notice how much you patience you have already, quietly waiting for a stoplight, calmly waiting for someone to figure out a solution to a problem you know inside and out. Two major things I recommend for developing patience is breathing deeply at times when you feel impatient. Like when you are late for work or school and you hit every red light. Or when someone just isn't getting what you are explaining to them. Breath deeply and be patient.

Today's Assignment:

Make yourself do nothing. Sit in front of a clock, no music, no movies, no games, no books, nothing but you and a clock. Sit quietly for 5 to 10 minutes. Time crawls like this, so try 5 minutes first. Develop the ability to sit quietly for extended periods of time, this will help. Practice sporadically throughout your training, this week and for the rest of your time as a Jedi. See if you can work up to 20 minutes of nothingness. I do not recommend over 30 minutes, unless you really need the break from life (or you are passenger in a very long car ride). Even then I recommend a hot bath or something relaxing over clock watching.

So - after the practice - How long did you do? How did it feel? Did time seem different? Did your mind race all over? Were you questioning the point of it all? How stupid the practice was? Update us, how did it go? Speak your mind.
Due Today.

The Five Traits - Day Three:
Objectivity

Objective thinking, there is simply no other way for a Jedi. A Jedi must take all sides into account, giving each person a fair hearing, and allow for all possibilities to exist. Bias, emotions, desire, these cannot be allowed to affect a Jedi's judgment. A Jedi must remain a fair neutral party in all that they do. By doing so they establish themselves as a Jedi (and order) that prizes justice, honesty, fairness, and objectiveness above all other things. Whether they like a person or not, whether they know the person is guilty for something else or not, if they are not the issue of the situation than they are not the issues which a Jedi focuses on.

In any situation people must be able to understand that a Jedi acts and bases their judgment upon clear logical facts and evidence. They are completely impartial, acting in a objective manner to bring a mutual resolution to the table. Adhering to local customs and laws and not allowing their own feelings and beliefs to interfere with any justice process.

One must understand that a Jedi's decisions are not based upon friendship or desire. Thus should a Jedi act against his friend, or disagree with him, it is important to note that it is nothing personal. It is simply logical fact which leads a Jedi to their conclusions. In this a Jedi is free to remove themselves from judgments and situations which have a conflict of interest. That is fair and objective as well. A Jedi must know when their presence and even judgment might compromise the validity and fairness of any given situation.

Another form of objective thinking is considering action. A Jedi has to accept that there is more than one outcome to a situation. They have to plan for success, failure, allies, opponents, and the many roads in between. Keeping a clear and open mind to the many possibilities that exist in any situation. A Jedi may take action, but also be prepared for the action to have many different consequences. If a Jedi merely thinks that they will walk into a situation and be able to resolve it, they are not thinking objectively and have already started to fail.

Evidence, facts, logic, reason, and listening to all parties in involved. Accepting the many outcomes of a situation, success, failure, and the variations. These are the keys to objective thinking. And yet this must also be applied to the Jedi themselves. A Jedi must be objective and honest with themselves if they expect to grow. They cannot believe themselves better than others or inferior to others just because. They must address themselves as everything else, looking at evidence, facts, and opinions. It is than that a Jedi can truly grow and strengthen their weaknesses.

Today's Assignment:

I want you to think of a recent situation in your life. Something that really got you going. Maybe really angry, or upset, sad, or even happy, or prideful. Just a recent event which really resulted in an emotional response (promotion at work, debate at school, someone cutting you off in traffic, or continually interrupting you).

Now think of yourself as an alien. Use your imagination, zoom out into space and look down upon the earth as if you were this alien. Observe all the happenings without any cares or bias that humans have - as if humans were ants. Look at our world as you would an ant farm.

Now I want you to consider that event, that situation, from that alien point of view. From this skyward position of simple observation. Re-examining the event from this context, does anything change? Do you pick on things you hadn't before? Considered possibilities that you may not have in the moment? Does this change your perception of the event and your reaction to it? Thoughts and insights - please share.
Due Today.

Part 2 -

Today you are going to promise to do something

tomorrow. A chore or something of that nature. Maybe something you have been putting off (or something you do not normally do). Washing dishes, mowing the lawn, dusting, giving a massage to your romantic partner, cleaning out the closet, making a doctor's appointment. Whatever it may be - make the promise - write it in your journal and tell someone it is relevant too. If bringing cupcakes to work tomorrow, inform the boss or something. Note: No cheating. No picking something you normally do. If tomorrow is your normal laundry day - no promising to do laundry. This should be something that requires a bit of extra effort on your part.

Today is just the informing us of what you will do tomorrow. So what is your promise for tomorrow?
Due Today.

The Five Traits - Day Four:
Reliability

Jedi are reliable, but what does this really mean? Does this mean a Jedi never fails, is never wrong, or never has to call in sick to work/school? Simply put it means one can rely on a Jedi to be a Jedi. Jedi are indeed trustworthy and reliable, but they do make mistakes, they do fail, and they are able to get sick. Yet when they call into school or work it is because they fully believe they would be more of a problem than an asset.

Jedi can be relied upon to be Jedi. Another circular phrase, which deserves a bit of explanation. Jedi, as we have seen hold to peace, knowledge, serenity, harmony, and the Force. And one can count on a Jedi to keep these core values close. Personally healthy, diplomatic, calm in stressful situations, these things are what Jedi are. And when one talks to an actual Jedi we can rely on the Jedi to be a model of these things and more. It is merely who Jedi are, what they represent.

Reliability for a Jedi comes in the fashion of Jedi keeping their word. A Jedi should promise little yet at the same deliver much more, as much as possible. In this a Jedi will be able to uphold their promises and set that standard of dependability, reliability. If a Jedi promises they will do something than they should do that and seek to go a step beyond. Again though you have to use common sense, in all duties, even charities, there are lines and boundaries. A Jedi should respect when doing more than requested would be a violation of trust or responsibility.

Also a Jedi must be relied upon to say no. A Jedi is not a doormat, a Jedi is not a slave, a Jedi is not a get out of work free card. People must rely on the Jedi to do what is necessary and trust they will back off when it is appropriate. A Jedi helps others, to help themselves. No individual, group, organization, or even government should ever come to depend solely on the Jedi. They must rely on the Jedi to help them (either an individual, group, organization, or government) become more capable and grow themselves. Jedi are not the means to an end, they are bridge to help others reach the end themselves.

Today's Assignment:
If you didn't see this coming, you need to work on that logic deduction. Yesterday you made a promise. Today it is to be delivered. Did you or did you not deliver on that promise?
Due Today.

And since that is an easy assignment. How about a little fun.
Three of these statements are untrue, so whodunnit?
Mr Red: "Mr Blue did it."
Mr Blue: "Mr Red did it."
Mr Green: "Mr Blue's telling the truth."
Mr Yellow: "Mr Green's not lying."
Due Today.

The Five Traits - Day Five:
Humility

Humility, has more than one meaning in relation to the Jedi. Many feel this simply states that a Jedi does not act arrogant, self-centered, and instead lowers him/herself to stay on the same level as everyone around them. Yet this is not exactly correct. While correct that a Jedi seeks to overcome arrogance and hold a view much broader than the self, a Jedi doesn't need to raise or lower themselves.

It is a simple fact is that the more you train to better yourself, the better you become over those that do not. This is simply how it works, those that work towards self-betterment become better. Knowing this is not arrogance, it is self-awareness, self-knowledge. A Jedi is better than others, because they train to be. But note - Better does not mean above or more important or more special.

Remember that we all have strengths and we all have weaknesses. While a Jedi may excel in one area, there are areas which others will be better at than yourself. Being a Jedi doesn't give an automatic ticket to being the best. There are people who train specifically in certain fields who will certainly be better in those fields. From Martial Arts to Medical Training to Fitness Experts.

As Jedi we seek world-betterment through self-betterment. In this we grow, evolve, and gain. We become better. Yet we have a very broad view. Physical, Emotional, Mental, Spiritual, and Social studies divide our time and attention. And while I am a decent boxer (I like/use boxing for self-defense and physical fitness), there are a plethora of individuals who can clean my clock, because Boxing is their life. They are simply better at it than me.

Humility is remembering, no matter what, there is always someone out there that is better than you. You may to meet them, but they are out there. To be at the top and stay there is about constant training, always striving to get to the next level. And even than - remember that person out there. The one who is a better cellist, one who is a better dancer, singer, writer, martial artist, grocery bagger.

In the end it comes down to a "So What?" mentality. So a Jedi is better in certain areas, so what? A Jedi understands that does not give them special privileges. Better, but still with the same friends, still needs to eat, wears clothes, bleeds when cut. A Jedi understands that self-betterment is not a ticket to special rights, honors, or privileges. So they continue to do what they do. They do the best they can in all they do. But they are not in it to gloat, to have the ego-stroked, to gain praise. They help those who request it, based upon logic, not skin color, religion, belief, et cetera. A Jedi is not looking to place themselves above others, they recognize that anyone can be as good as them if they merely trained to be. It is merely matter of training.

The Power of the Jedi book states, "*A Jedi is a Jedi only because someone else has taken the trouble to teach them.*" Because you have taken the time to live and learn as a Jedi. It is an effort on all our parts and is not accomplished alone. "*<u>The acceptance of others is not a guarantee. Like everyone else, a Jedi is accepted or not based on his behavior The Jedi who believes that he is more important than others only demonstrates that his opinion is to be ignored.</u>*" - Power of the Jedi, quoting Dooku (during his Jedi storyline).

It is important to understand that as Jedi we must be honest and accept who we are and our talents and abilities. At the same time we must recognize that these simply make us different. This does not place us above anyone, it simply denotes and highlights the training we have undertaken. Jedi are not doormats and we are not tyrants. We are not above, nor are we below. That can be forgotten when we begin to notice that we have a different view and understanding of the world than some of those around us.

Today's Assignment:
No doubt there is something you excel at. But did you get there on your own? I want you to take a moment and reflect on all the little things as well as people that helped you excel at -enter your awesomeness here-. Whether paintball king, looked to as a expert in grammar, teacher in martial arts. Whatever it is, share your mastery and than share some of the people and things that helped make it possible.

The Five Traits - Day Six:
Wisdom

While Jedi seek to preserve of knowledge, they understand that it takes wisdom to use knowledge properly. While Jedi are seen as wise, they merely work from knowledge, experience, and the Force. Wisdom we can say is the combination of knowledge + experience.

A Jedi gains wisdom and knowledge by being mindful; mindful of themselves, their surroundings, environment, feelings, and how all things these tend to link together. Where we live, who we hang out with, our family, all things things have an effect on us. As Jedi we must be aware of this and seek to overcome the hurdles in our lives.

Through our experience in life we gain the wisdom of life. Likewise as we progress as Jedi we gain wisdom into the Jedi lifestyle. Wisdom is a fancy and overrated way of saying "been there, done that." Truly wisdom is simply the combination of our accumulated knowledge and our experiences with said knowledge.

It is said that wisdom is to know something deeply. To be enlightened about a certain subject (whether that subject be life or automobiles). It is one thing to know that placing your hand in a fire will hurt. It is another to know the exact process, exactly what happens and what it does. In this wisdom you know how to avoid it. "I have to place my hand in the fire to grab that ring. I know via knowledge and experience that if I drench my hand in water that I have more time without being burned. I know via knowledge and experience my long sleeves will catch fire so I'll remove those. I know via knowledge and experience that metal ring will be extremely hot and will need to hold it with something." In this you can create the best approach to retrieving the ring from the fire. And one watching may praise your wisdom in the matter.

This is what it means to be wise as a Jedi. That you have studied, you have trained, you have observed, you have experienced (even gained the experience of others), and are able to consider the most possible scenarios in the least possible time, with the best possible outcomes/options. And the more you exercise this the more wisdom you gain from it (even in mistakes and failures). The more you work on wisdom the more you gain it.

Wisdom comes to us everyday. From knowing the best ways to get to work/school, to how best to deal with a friend in any given situation. We can rely on our own personal skills/abilities, our knowledge of the situation, and our previous experiences to get us through. And when we lack in one f those, it is rather easy correct. And in the end, by just taking that leap forward we can be sure we will gain the wisdom for the next time (or how to avoid a next time).

Today's Assignment:
Hit me with some wisdom. I want at least one (no more than two - limited time and all) life wisdom given. With it, I want a personal example/experience to accompany it. So ensure it has, Knowledge, Experience, and is something that you believe will benefit myself or others. Hit Me King Solomon.

The Five Traits - Day Seven:
Main Assignment

Today's Assignment:
Example Time - Remember This?
Give a personal example of when your patience was tested and you remained patient - During This Week.
Give a personal example of when you were objective - During This Week. Personal example of when you were counted on and were proven reliable - During This Week. Personal example of being humble - This Week. And last but not least personal example of exercising wisdom - During This Week.
Due Today.

The Jedi Rules of Behavior - Day One:
Overview.

The Jedi Rules of Behavior were written for the Star Wars tabletop role-playing, specifically the Jedi companion books, thus a fictional source. They first appear in the Power of the Jedi RPG companion guide. They go a bit further on specifics than the Jedi Code. As we look at the Jedi Rules of Behavior we are going to keep this as short as possible. The overview will be simply a list. And we will break them up and tackle them in groups over the course of the week. Even in this I'll look to not overload you talking about them.

    I just want you to get a feel for the Jedi Rules of Behavior and applying them to your everyday life. To have a core and basic understanding of these rules, why the exist, and how they enforce the Jedi Path. We will look at the fictional description of each element and then look at the reality of the rule given. How it applies to us rather than how it applies to our fictional counterparts.

    As you can see (and will see once we list all the rules) the Jedi have a lot elements they juggle at once. It can even seem overwhelming at times. The important thing to remember is that you have time. Rome wasn't built in a day and no one mastered being a Jedi in a month. These things take time and repetition to sink in and become second nature.

    Yet it is important for you to get a sense of all that applies to the Jedi Path and living as a Jedi. In this you can see what to expect from the leadership here. What we expect from you as a Jedi (with a learning curve and time to adjust of course - you will stumble, that is okay, all part of the learning process). And gives you things to work on (and be mindful of) during your time as a Jedi.

    Tier One is a bit of an information overload with all the

new things we throw at you. And assignments we have you do nearly everyday. Things slow down in the up tiers a bit. There is much more focus on singular concepts to help you really get each individual element down and applied to your every day life. This way Jedi training takes a long time. Why it cannot be done in six months to a year. No one claiming to be a Jedi Knight or Jedi Master who went through six months or a year of training has earned that. In fact I doubt most Jedi would feel comfortable with such a title until after at least five continual, non-stop years of training.

That is the type of journey you have ahead of you and why we do not use titles here. It is about living and being a Jedi. Not some title you picked up on the way to the store. I have been at this for a decent amount of time and I would not place such titles on myself. It is simply about living and being a Jedi - everyday, the best you can. Do that and you'll always have the highest respect, regardless of title/label.

Now - Jedi Rules of Behavior that we will be covering:
1 Self-Discipline:
2 Conquer Arrogance:
3 Conquer Overconfidence:
4 Conquer Defeatism:
5 Conquer Stubbornness:
6 Conquer Recklessness:
7 Conquer Curiosity:
8 Conquer Aggression:
9 Conquer External Loyalties:
10 Conquer Materialism:
11 Responsibility:
12 Practice Honesty:
13 Honor Your Promises:
14 Honor the Jedi Order:
15 Honor the Law:
16 Honor Life:
17 Public Service:
18 Render Aid:

19 Defend the Weak
20 Provide Support:

-= Lesson Four Assignment One =-
Incorporating Jedi Practices into Your Life - Daily. Part Two
NOTE: <u>These are not to replace or be replaced by your current studies and activities.</u> Meaning, if you already do a specific meditation, you are still to practice what is listed here. If you work-out and cover these exercises you are still to do them at some point. <u>These are supplemental exercises for daily use</u>, to be used in conjunction with your current lifestyle.

- <u>Physical Fitness</u> - Start with some light stretching (touch the toes, reaching for the sky, etc.). A little knee high marching in place. Now - 20 Lunges, 20 Hip Raises, 20 Mountain Climbers, 15 Push-up with Arm Reach, 20 Squats, 20 V-ups, and 20 Burpees. Daily, Once, any time; I recommend morning right when you get out of bed. 10 minutes should give you enough time to knock these out. Pictures At the End. As a side-note, you can rest, mid-set break if needed, but accomplish the numbers given and seek to push through.

- <u>Meditation</u> - The Mind-Body Approach (by Dr. Herbert Benson)

Step 1: Choose a meaningful word or short phrase that can be repeated silently on a single exhalation, or outbreath. From shalom, to Christ, to Peace, or Calm. Consider a word that you feel best represents your view and goal of relaxation.

Step 2: Assume a comfortable sitting position, close your eyes, breathe easily and regularly, and repeat your chosen word or phrase silently on the outbreath for fifteen minutes. Use and set an alarm for this (doable with most cell phones). Seek to use a soft chime - nothing harsh, but something to gently let you know the time is up (music if able).

Step 3: Don't fight or be upset with distracting thoughts or interruptions. It's normal for your mind to wander, especially when you are just getting used to this exercise. The important thing is not to become uptight or begin to feel you have failed. Rather, just sigh and say silently, "oh well," and return to the repetition.
Step 4: After the allotted fifteen minutes have passed, open your eyes, sit quietly for five minutes, and allow everyday thoughts to enter your mind. You can clock watch here, don't need an alarm. Just give yourself a few minutes to get back into daily life.

- <u>Awareness</u> - Take a moment and just take in your surroundings. Above you, behind you, to the sides, below, just look around, note the things you see.

- <u>Diplomacy</u> - Another key part of diplomacy is objectivity. We have looked at compromise - hopefully enforcing that win/win approach. We have looked at the importance of not only our own tone of voice, but also ensuring tone does not distract us (yet recognizing its use). All this is seeking to build to objectivity, to keep us grounded in the information gathering mode without placing our own ego into the ring. A tough thing, to remove ourselves and keep that objective bird's eye view. Yet that is our practice this week - which should be easy given lesson last week. Seek the objective bird's eye view in your dealings with week.

- <u>Self-Discipline</u> - Get it done. All of it. No excuses. Even if life gets crazy, these things are easy to keep up with. So keep on it.

Today's Assignment:
Looking only at the list in the lesson. Which "rules" do you think you'll have the most issues with? Which ones are you looking forward to learning more about? Which ones do you feel

don't fit into the daily life of a Jedi? Include your reasoning on all please. Also - find and share a link where you can read the Jedi Rules of Behavior online.
Due Today.

Exercise Pictures:
Lunges: Stand, comfortably, extend one leg forward, bending at the knee. Do Not let your other knee hit the ground. Stand back up, alternate legs.

Hip Raise: Lay with your back flat on the ground with knees bent - as if doing sit-ups. Now simply raise your hips off the ground while keeping your shoulders on the ground. Creating a straight diagonal line from knees to shoulders.

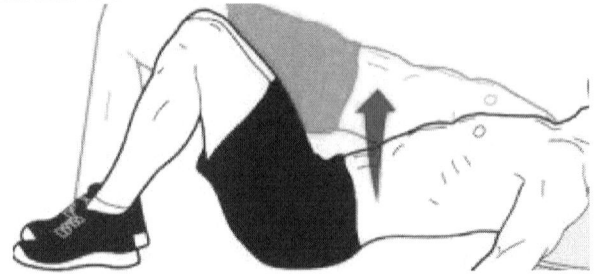

Mountain Climbers: Get into the starting Push-up Position. Now, you push off with your leg, bring the knee into the chest, while the other leg stays extended. Kick your leg back and bring the other knee into the chest.

Push-up with Arm Reach: Normal Push-up with the addition that when you reach the up position lift one arm up; fingertips going to the sky.

Squats: Normal Squat - should have this one down by now.

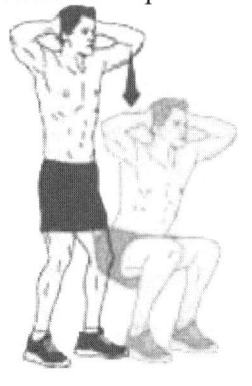

V-ups: Lay on your back, flat on the ground. Arms extended above your head. Legs out straight. Bring your arms over and in front of you, reaching toward your toes. At the same time lift your legs up. And bringing your shoulders and back off the floor. Lay back down bringing your arms back over your head.

Burpee: Stand up straight. Squat down, kick your feet out so you are in the Push-up position. Do a Push-up. Bring your feet back in. Stand up.

The Rules – Day Two:
First Five

::Self-Discipline::

Fictional - Self-Discipline is one of the key factors of Jedi behavior, and many lessons taught to the Jedi from the beginning focus on this basic doctrine. As the Jedi grows, the lessons increase in complexity to emphasize the importance of a disciplined life. The Jedi learns that self-discipline is one of the more important lessons to be learned and it will serve her well throughout her life.

Reality - Self-discipline is required to complete any task or goal we desire. Whether that be to climb the corporate ladder, to running that marathon, or simply enjoying some needlepoint. No one is going to force us to excel and succeed in life and in truth no one can force us. We have to find that inner drive ourselves to complete what we start. And each of us, no matter who you are, no matter what excuses you can think of or have taught of before, we have this discipline to see things through.

That is why this is listed as a cornerstone of Jedi philosophy, because without it we would accomplish nothing. Guess what, if you want something bad enough, you will get it done, you will prioritize, you will find that self-discipline whether you fully recognize it or not. Jedi, like any other thing in life, requires we focus and finish what we start.

::Conquer Arrogance::

Fictional - Jedi train to be different, but their training and abilities do not make them better than other people. A Jedi is only a Jedi because someone else has taken the trouble to teach them. Dooku once said, *"The acceptance of others is not a guarantee. Like everyone else, a Jedi is accepted or not based on his behavior. The Jedi who believes that he is more important than others only demonstrates that his opinion is to be ignored."*

Reality - Arrogance for a Jedi denotes an over-abundance. It creates a blind spot in which we fail recognize certain truths. Such as none of us were born special, none of us are greater than others, we are all the same on the inside, our blood is the same color. We have done nothing special, Jedi haven't achieved something beyond anyone else. We took the time and made the effort and if it weren't for the many teachers in our lives we wouldn't be where we are.

A Jedi acknowledges the full truth, we note their skills, abilities, and strengths. They also note their weaknesses, the people who have helped them along the way, and the simple fact anyone could walk their road if they chose. Don't let your accomplishments blind you to reality.

::Conquer Overconfidence::

Fictional - As a Jedi's training progresses, they can start to take on the behavior that they can do anything with their abilities. Jedi instructors teach these students to realize their limits so that they can accurately measure how far they can go, as well as understand their own limitations. Vodo-Siok said, "*Overconfident thinking is flawed because the Jedi does not take all possibilities into account. he may understand the task at hand, the support of his fellows, and the ramifications of his success, and he may have even planned for unanticipated factors-but he has failed to understand his own capabilities. He has planned only for success, because he has concluded that there can be no failure. Every Jedi, in every task, should prepare for the possibility of failure.*"

Reality - Again we are looking at an over-abundance. We all note that confidence is a good and needed thing. Even some arrogance is needed at times. But for Jedi it is about balance, it is about objectivity. A Jedi must recognize their faults along with their strengths. Take note of your skills, abilities, understand what you excel at, but also keep in mind the areas you are ignorant, where you need improvement. In this we can properly plan and react to events which cater to our strengths and weaknesses.

In acknowledging these things we can know when it is

better to let someone else lead. We can better determine when it is best to sit back and be supportive and when it is best to take the lead and offer direction.

::Conquer Defeatism::

Fictional - The opposite of overconfidence is defeatism; the belief that no effort, no matter how great, can possibly succeed. It amounts to a matter of priorities. A Jedi should plan for success before contemplating failure. The Jedi who plans excessively for failure expects to lose. Indeed, the Jedi who approaches each task as though failure is the most likely option puts forth only the minimal effort; enough to say that she tried.

Reality - Balance. Defeatism tends to happen when we focus too much on the what ifs, when we give too much credit to our weaknesses and not enough to the reality of our strengths. Giving-up is something we have all done at some point. Sometimes it is truly the best and most beneficial option. Sometimes it allows us to let go, collect ourselves, and refocus on something better, something beneficial to ourselves and others.

I have had to give-up on things which was every difficult to do, but you come to a point where you must weigh the options carefully, honestly, objectively. And it is in these moments that you cannot allow defeatism or depression, to color your judgment and determine your decision. It must be made with clarity and integrity.

::Conquer Stubbornness::

Fictional - A Jedi who focuses too much on a single goal or perspective loses sight of other possibilities, including ones that might yield better results. A Jedi must learn that staying on one path or clinging to one point of view can be costly. A Jedi must keep her mind open and not be afraid to change with the situation. A Jedi should be willing to accept defeat if the cost of winning is greater than the cost of losing. Rekpa De said, "*Do not see a duel as a choice between winning and losing. Every duel can have many, many outcomes. When you concentrate solely on* *winning-as in everything else-you sully your victory. Winning becomes worse than losing. It is better to lose well than to win badly. And it is always better to end a duel peacefully than to win or lose."*

Reality - Again we are noting an imbalance. A Jedi needs determination, they need to be able to hold their ground, this is core in life. If we are not able to stick to our beliefs they become worthless. However, we must be willing to examine our beliefs, we must be willing to examine our stance, the very ground we are standing on. In this we can ensure our beliefs are worth holding on to, that they are worth standing firm for.

We must be open to the various possibilities in life. When given a choice in option A or option B, we need to look for a valid option C. Sometimes we need to let go, change ideas, tactics, change our view, and we have to be open to that possibility. Finding the balance of honesty, objectivity, reason, to help determine where we place our beliefs and hold our ground.

-= Lesson Four - Day Two Assignment =-

For each of these subjects. I want you to write of a time when they were beneficial and a time when it was not the right call. Example - A time Stubbornness was a useful and beneficial action. Now a time when it was not.

If you cannot think of an example, of a time when it was beneficial or not, simply say so. You won't lose anything. If the example is too personal to share in a public journal, simply say so, but that you did think of a time when it was or was not beneficial.

Due *by* Tomorrow.

The Rules – Day Three:
Second Five

::Overcome Recklessness::

Fictional - Young Jedi in particular perceive a goal and rush towards it, heedless of the unseen dangers or other options. Wiwa said, *"Learn to recognize when speed is not important. Race when being first is important; move at your own pace at all other times. It is not necessary to always strike the first blow, to provide the first solution, or to reach a goal before anyone else does. In fact, it is sometimes vital to strike the last blow, to give the final answer, or to arrive after everyone else."*

Reality - Patience, it is core to the Jedi. Rushing is not always the best option. Haste is rarely the answer. How many times when in a rush do we forget simple things? Keys, an important paper, jacket, a gift. We find ourselves late, we rush, we overlook, forget, and find ourselves even more behind. Going full-steam ahead into a brick wall, what good does it serve of us?

Again we can denote times when we have to throw caution to wind, muster the courage to be a little reckless. Yet for a Jedi, mostly we are talking about being patient, observant, about understanding that by letting our recklessness take over we often blind ourselves to the small details which are vital and necessary. Thus we seek to balance that with patience.

::Conquer Curiosity::

Fictional - All people, no matter how public their lives are entitled to their privacy. It is unseemly for a Jedi to probe unnecessarily into the business of others. All beings are entitled to their privacy, and intruding gives the clear message that the privacy of others can be sacrificed to satisfy a Jedi's curiosity. To discreetly uncover the secrets of others might be occasionally necessary, but it should never be a matter of course, for it causes distrust of the Jedi in general. Odan-Urr said, "Use the Force to satisfy the will of the Force; not to satisfy your own curiosity."

Reality - Humans tend to be very curious creatures. As Jedi we need to make sure we are not crossing privacy lines for our own personal sake. This comes into play when helping others, this doesn't really apply to training or learning. Some areas it is important to ask questions, be curious, nurture that desire for knowledge and growth. As Jedi we need to recognize when it important, when it is beneficial to ask questions and indulge our curiosity, and when it is counter-productive. Unless truly necessary delving into someone's personal life is unbecoming of a Jedi.

We all have areas which are our own business. Learn to recognize the relevant from the idle curiosity. This is simply a reminder of personal boundaries. That digging too deeply for purely curiosity sake can be considered rude and counter-productive.

::Conquer Aggression::

Fictional - For those less experienced in the ways of the Jedi, knowing the difference between attack, defense, and aggression does not come easily. A Jedi can attack without aggression, especially if she is calm, at peace, and not filled with anger or hatred. However, a Jedi must explore every alternative before employing violent, harmful, and/or lethal force.

Reality - Aggression can manifest itself in a variety of ways. It is not just about physical aggression, but also emotional, and verbal aggression. Sometimes you need to be assertive to get ahead. In life, in your career, in school work, in a race (Spartan race definitely). Meaning that you need to press forward with determination and confidence. If you passively sit back you'll be pushed aside, stepped on, and ignored. Being assertive is necessary to ensure that you are not a doormat. But check that to make sure that it does not become aggressiveness. Personally I find the two differ in perspective. When your judgment is clouded and you are pressing ahead with tunnel vision - you are aggressive. When you are pushing ahead, but open to various possibilities, keeping an objective view, you are being assertive.

This is a reminder to find the balance, the line. Not aggression, assertiveness. Not anger, not indignation, not blind faith. We as Jedi cannot allow ourselves to be blinded by the finish-line. Yes, we want to excel, to succeed, but we must also always be aware at what cost. Be calm and at peace within so that you may move seamlessly - attacking the problem when needed - without aggression or anger or hate. Instead seek the best for all involved, sometimes that means coming in second.

::Conquer External Loyalties::

Fictional - Hoche Trit said: "*A Jedi is a Jedi, first, foremost, and only. For a Jedi to divide his attention between the will of the Force and the will of others is to invite disaster.*" A Jedi is free to have connections with others outside the Path, but divided loyalties can compromise a Jedi's effectiveness. Other loyalties can distract him from the task at hand and cause undue hardship for others. A Jedi's loyalties should lie with the Force, the Jedi Order, and himself, in that order.

Reality - Family. Friends. Career. School. We are not a monastic order in a galaxy far far away. We do not get government funding. We cannot dedicate our lives to training and spending dedicated team to tackle problems. We have daily commitments which require our time, our energy, our resources, our loyalty. We must provide for our family. We want to be there and enjoy time with our friends. If we do not honor our commitments to our school and/or job we will not have the resources/means to support ourselves (and enjoy those first two elements).

So what does this mean? Conquer External Loyalties? Simple. Do not be blinded. Keep an open and objective mind. Learn to recognize when one of these commitments is destroying you. Would you suggest someone stay in an abusive relationship simply out of loyalty to the person? Loyalty is a great and noble concept, but one must be mindful that it is not being used as an anchor.

Likewise - living as a Jedi takes commitment. Just like school, just like work, just like friends, we require some of your time and loyalty as well. You are going to have a conflict of interest arise and you must choose where to invest your time and energy. Look at it objectivity. Be mindful, consider what works best for you, what goal you are seeking to reach, what will help you, and move forward. If that is school, work, family, and/or friends (which it often is), then you move in that direction.

To be clear this isn't a one or the other. Simply a reminder that you *will* have to prioritize your time and you need to stay mindful when doing so. Going out drinking with your friends instead of fulfilling your commitments because of loyalty to your friends - not a Jedi endorsed practice.

::Conquer Materialism::

Fictional - Like external loyalties, possessions can also be a distraction. A Jedi doesn't need to lead a ascetic life, but she learns to travel light, carrying with her only the bare essentials. Very few Jedi own more than what they can carry. In the words of Kagoro: "*I wear my robe so that I am warm; I carry my lightsaber that I am safe; and I keep enough credits for my next meal, so that I am not hungry. If the Force wants me to have more, it finds a way of letting me know.*"

Reality - A reminder of perspective. Fancy toys and high-end items are nice, but are they necessary? Some people care a lot about the material. I certainly enjoy it, but I lean towards the minimal. A nice little house, my own little car, things that help me fulfill my commitments in life. Computer, internet so I can be here. But I enjoy luxuries - X-Box 360 to blow off steam and connect with my friends over long distance. I enjoy buying nice things for my friends and girlfriend. I am spoiled and like to spoil others in my life.

Here is the crux. It is not about being a monk and having nothing. It is about being able to let go at any moment. If your place is on fire, do not risk your life to save your material things. Computer, 360, none of that is worth your life. When someone puts a gun in your face for your watch and shoes - give it to them. Not worth dying over. It is just stuff. Do not let material things become your focus, your purpose. Understand they are nice to have, but do not let them define you. Let you, your beliefs, your actions, you ability define who you are - not some plastic junk that will be obsolete in three years.

Materialistic nature has its place. Supporting yourself in society and having a house, a car (or living somewhere where you do not need a car), these are great things to strive for. Shelter, Food, Water, Clothing. Support yourself, but when you start wasting grocery money on game subscriptions, that is a problem.

-= Lesson Four - Day Three Assignment =-

For each of these subjects. I want you to write of a time when they were beneficial and a time when it was not the right call. Example - A time Stubbornness was a useful and beneficial action. Now a time when it was not.

If you cannot think of an example, of a time when it was beneficial or not, simply say so. You won't lose anything. If the example is too personal to share in a public journal, simply say so, but that you did think of a time when it was or was not beneficial. **Due by Tomorrow.** Sound familiar? How boring. Oh well. Get to it bored Jedi.

The Rules – Day Four:
Third Five

::Responsibility::

Fictional - Once the ideals of self-discipline are learned, a Jedi can begin taking responsibility for his actions. Any Jedi that does not take responsibility for his actions lacks the discipline expected of him as a member of the Jedi Order. No Jedi who shuns responsibility should be trained, and no Jedi who embraces responsibility should be denied training.

Reality - Responsibility. Accountability. Integrity. If you cannot accept these things as a core part of your being - bow out now. I have watched people destroy lives, crush people, all for selfish desires. They refused to face their mistakes, they shunned their responsibility, they denied the damage they caused. Self-righteous sanctimonious complete disregard for all personal and organizational responsibility. If I see this in anyone who dares calls themselves a Jedi - you are gone.

Don't lie. You screw up, own up. You cut a corner and are asked about it, accept responsibility. Be accountable for your actions. You know how many mistakes I have made in my life? As a person? As a Jedi? Too many. I own it, I do not ask forgiveness, I simply seek to do what I can to make it right, to make amends, to adjust the situation back into a beneficial light. But all I can do is control me - all I have power over is myself.

Accept responsibility for Yourself. Your Actions, Your Reactions, Your Words. Do not accept responsibility for others. Exceptions being leadership, and others might include parenting in that. But again - not all responsibility. Accept your Part. Do not carry the weight of the world on your shoulders. Be objectivity, be smart, accept what is yours and let others accept or deny what is theirs.

Responsibility. Accountability. Integrity. You are not a Jedi without these things.

::Practice Honesty::

Fictional - Honesty is the first responsibility of the Jedi, and recognizing its importance is vital to becoming a valued member of the Order. Although certain situations might require a Jedi to stretch the truth or create falsehoods within a particular situation, a Jedi must remain honest with himself, his Master, and the Council. Continually creating lies or subjecting others to delusions invites suspicion and incites anger from others upon discovery of truth. *"Let there be truth between your heart and the Force. All else is transitory."*

Reality - Self-Honesty is core. Open and Honest Communication is key in any relationship - especially with any Mentor/Instructor you may have. Not everyone is deserving of this and sometimes you will need to keep things close to the vest. My advice, what I live by, *"never say more than you have too."* If you do not want to lie and you do not want to say than don't. Stick with neutral non-committal comments. But always maintain that honesty with yourself. Do not lie to yourself, do not lie to those you trust and have allowed to be close to you.

Honesty is the best policy. We stick to that. It goes hand-and-hand with Responsibility, Accountability, and Integrity. But truth carries weight and it is not a burden to throw around lightly. You must be mindful of the consequences of just slinging your truth around. You must be aware that a lot of things are subjective. Now we aren't going to tell you how answer when a friend asks if you like their new hairstyle. People's feelings and ego are fragile. Personally I like to look for truthful nice things I can say and go with that. But generally speaking, Jedi policy is self-honesty first and foremost. What you chose to share with others is a decision you must make, hopefully based upon responsibility and integrity.

::Honor Your Promises::

Fictional - A Jedi that makes a promise should be prepared to follow through with that promise or make amends, if necessary. One who makes promises that he does not intend to keep creates dishonesty and is less likely to be trusted. Tho-Mes Drei said: "*Deliver more than you promise. The best way to be always certain of this is to deliver much, even when you promise nothing.*"

Reality - It is simple. Do What You Say You Will Do. Easy as that. If you have trouble with that, like myself, than shut your mouth until you can be 100%. I bury myself in all the things I want to do. I want to help, I want to write this, create that, school, work, charities, online stuff, promises to friends, I overload my plate and things fall off. I forget commitments I had made. All a no-no. So I had to adjust, I had to re-evaluate my speech patterns, my quick nature of committing myself to projects. I had to remove myself because I had simply given too much.

Now, I promise little and do what I can when I can. In this I can provide services and extras without burying myself. I am not stressed out because this deadline is due with five things at once. I can calmly and quietly work on and complete promises at my leisure because fifty of them aren't waiting on me to finish the fifty others I am working on. So it is that simple. Do What You Say - Don't Say More Than You Have Too - Keep Your Word. All ties to Accountability, Reliability, Responsibility, et cetera.

::Honor the Jedi Order::

Fictional - A Jedi's words and actions represent the Order as a whole. Positive words and deeds reflect positively, while negative ones damage the Order's reputation. Billions of people inhabit our world, and only a tiny fraction of them have ever encountered a Jedi. The words and deeds of a single Jedi often create a first (and often lasting) impression of the Order as a whole. Odan-Urr reflected: "*When a Jedi behaves badly in public, an observer might think, 'If this Jedi is representative of the whole Order, than plainly no Jedi is worthy of respect.' It would take many encounters with other, more behaved Jedi to undo the mistakes of one.*"

Reality - Everything - EVERYTHING - you say and do

represents the Jedi as a whole. You speak for me. You speak for all Jedi. Your actions, reactions, words, they speak for all Jedi past, present, future. Please respect that. This applies to all of us. I speak for you. Do not go around saying keeping your hoodie up is your religious right. That is speaking for every Jedi everywhere. When you go out partying with friends - Guess what? Still speaking for all Jedi everywhere? Lie, cheat, steal, you are saying all Jedi condone this action and live that way.

You are a Jedi. You carrying the reputation of the entire Jedi Order with you. As you would not want other Jedi to go around saying prayers to Yoda, wearing robes, and swinging plastic lightsabers claiming to be Jedi Masters. Act as you would like Jedi to be recognized as. Honor yourself, honor the name, honor the Jedi as a whole.

::Honor the Law::

Fictional - For the Jedi to protect peace and justice, the Jedi must be held to those same local laws; Jedi uphold its laws, ideals, and protect its citizens, thus are bound by it. When traveling outside the local areas and country, a Jedi must exercise extreme care, for local governments might operate differently than their own customs, and a incident in which the Jedi breaks local laws is an extremely unpleasant one. And he must then be prepared to accept the consequences of his actions.

Reality - Unless it is your actual job, Jedi are not Police Officers, we certainly are not vigilantes, we are not Judges, we are not the Law. It is not the role of the Jedi to enforce the law. It is the role of the Jedi to support the law. To honor the law. Be a good witness, take detailed notes, inform the proper authorities who have the proper training and legal status to act accordingly. Learn the Law - learn about good Samaritan laws, learn about citizen arrest laws, learn what your local police would like you to do in the event of a crime taking place. Educate yourself and support the system. Make it work.

Don't go around breaking the law. This ties into honoring the Jedi. Yes there are exceptions to every point, don't go looking for it. Don't try to justify anything. Self-Honesty remember? Instead simply seek to support and follow the local laws. Don't take the law into your own hands. Honor the law.

-= Lesson Four - Day Four Assignment =-

Basically the same as before. But we need to make adjustments due to the nature of the points here.

1.) How have you been responsible? When did you hold yourself accountable? How did that work for you? Likewise, was there a time when you ducked responsibility and accountability? How did that work out for you?

2.) Same with honesty. Time you were open and honest. A time you lied freely. How did those work out?

3.) Promises - A time you held yourself to it. A time you failed to keep your promise. Getting the theme here?

4.) Honoring the Jedi Order. Think of a time you feel represented the Jedi well. How about a time that would not be so favorable?

5.) The Law. We'll let this one go. Do **not** tell me your transgressions in this area. Simply acknowledge that you understand and will seek to honor and follow this concept to the best of your ability.

The Rules – Day Five:
Fourth Five

::Honor Life::

Fictional - Since life is what strengthens the Force, honoring life in all forms is one of the highest priorities of the Jedi Order. Care must be taken to protect life and avoid unnecessary death. If a situation arises where a life must be taken after all other options have been contemplated, a Jedi should make sure that the reason is justified. Typically, this should be done in self-defense or the defense of others incapable of defending themselves. A Jedi should never assume that the taking of a life is no cause for concern.

Reality - Honor Life. Respect it. Protect it. Not many of us will be in a position of actual life-and-death situations (thankfully). Some will, some Jedi are Police Officers, some Soldiers, and they'll have to face this and act accordingly (defend themselves and ensure they go home to their loved ones), which is tough. But for the rest of us we find this in our daily choices. I know one Jedi those chose to stop killing spiders. She is terrified of them, but now makes the effort to get them outside when they cross paths.

For some they take this and go a vegan or vegetarian route in life. This is not what this means per se, but it is an acceptable translation. Some feel simply going organic is the best approach. *shrugs* I feel it translate to respect your life, your families life. That has a two-fold meaning. First respecting the freedom of choice of living beings. Second, respect life. Seek means of enforcing life, encouraging it. This is often found in a healthy lifestyle. Supporting and strengths life - not cutting it short.

I don't see stuffing double-quarter pounders with cheese, large fries, and a soda down every day as honoring life. I see that as chipping away at life. At the same time, I do not believe one should deny themselves their own pleasures of life. Running in mud obstacle races is dangerous. Bungee jumping, parachuting, all dangerous and potentially life shortening. Yet, honoring life isn't about hiding in a closet trying to live as long as possible. It is about embracing life, enjoying life, getting the most out of life. Again though, I do not see McFatty's as embracing and enjoying life, but that is just my personal view. Honor Life, do what you feel best fulfills this. Life is short enough. Embrace it. For me that means telling the ones you love that you love them. It means not sitting inside letting life pass you by. It is about getting out there and doing and living. And enjoying the occasional foods which are "horrible" for you. I love desserts - so I definitely partake. The joys of life in my opinion and the benefit of working out everyday, I can indulge.

You must find your way to honor life. Be honest, be objective, be mindful, and really seek to honor life in a positive and beneficial manner.

::Public Service::

Fictional - While the Jedi exist to study the ways of the Force, they are allowed to exist because they serve the public interest. Were they unable to use the Force- indeed, if the Force did not exist- the Jedi would go on serving, because this is their mandate. The fact that the Force is real, and that the Jedi are its most devoted practitioners, only strengths their resolve to use it in the service of the common good.

Reality - I really just want to leave that as is. Re-read it. Again. There it is. I mean, I highly doubt we are the Force's most devoted practitioners, but that section really just says it all. What one must understand is that public service and all various related topics on the matter, a Jedi is not the end all solution. As Jedi Joshua once said: "*We help others help themselves.*" A Jedi understands it is important to aid to others, yet more important to help them aid themselves. Teach one to fish, don't just throw fish at them. Outside of that I got nothing here. Re-read it. Yes, again. There it is.

::Render Aid::

Fictional - A Jedi is obligated to assist those in need of aid whenever possible, and must be able to quickly judge the priority of doing so. Saving one life is important; saving multiple lives more so. This tenet does not require a Jedi abandon other goals in every circumstance, but the Jedi must do her best to ensure that those in need of aid receive it.

((Updated Version: In conjunction with promoting the ideals of the light side of the Force, all Jedi endeavor to provide aid to those in need whenever possible. However, a Jedi should not forgo his other ideals to do so.))

Reality - All Jedi endeavor to provide aid to those in need whenever possible. This can take place in a variety of ways. We explore this concept through the five goals of the Jedi. We reminder ourselves that we must service and a part of that is rendering aid to those in need. How is a question of many answers. We see many groups which provide a good answer and by lending our aid to them we strengthen our ability to send aid on a global scale. It is a simple and short concept - be in a position to help others. Here, be capable of providing aid to those in need - in whatever way you can.

::Defend the Weak::

Fictional - A Jedi should strive to defend the weak against those who seek to oppress them, from one person suffering at the hands of another to an entire race held in thrall. A Jedi should always remember, though, that not all might be as it seems. The customs of other cultures should always be respected, even if they offend the Jedi's moral or ethical code. In every case, though, the Jedi should carefully consider the ramifications of her actions. Master Marspa sighed. "*Were it within my authroity on Nal Hutta, I would have set every last slave free and personally escorted them back home to their loved ones, far from Hutt space. But to interfere with the culture of the Hutts on their homeworld would have been to pass judgment on them on behalf of the Republic.*

The Republic Senate knows that slavery goes on in Hutt space. When they decide to do something about that, I will support them wholeheartedly.
On the other hand, slavery is not legal on Ord Mantell. For that shopkeeper to beat his employee was simply an unnecessary display of dominance. Were the Republic aware of his actions, they would have acted immediately. I am sad that there is a difference between the two, but it is not our place to correct the discrepancy."

((Updated Version: A Jedi should strive to defend those who are unable to defend themselves. At the same time, a Jedi must be aware that what might seem to be oppression in one culture might not necessarily be so in another. The morals and ethics of other cultures need to be carefully considered before taking action, lest a Jedi insinuate herself into a situation where her help is not desired.))

Reality - Jedi study and train to be strong capable individuals. In a position to defend themselves, to stickup for themselves, to be fully comfortable with who they are. Not all have this solid sense of self. And some that do end up lording it over others who do not. Jedi can and are encouraged to lend their strength and understanding to those that have not yet discovered their own strength yet. The five goals explores the many ways we can act here. But again we come back to the core ideal of ensuring self-reliance over depending on the Jedi.

If you stop the bully, that is good. But what has the person being bullied learned? It is not just about the oppressor. It is about educating, encouraging, and supporting those who are being picked on, being oppressed. They must make the conscious choice to stand up for themselves. They must find the beauty, strength, and courage within themselves. A Jedi can help in this and certainly a Jedi can defend them and give them the time they need to reach that realization. Remember it is not always about physical defense, the emotional can have a much more lasting effect.

::Provide Support::

Fictional - At times, a Jedi must stand aside to let others render aid or defend the weak - even though the Jedi could perhaps do a better job. The Jedi should assist by word or by action as required by the situation, offering advice when asked for, warning when necessary, and argument only when reason fails. Otherwise, the Jedi must remember that she wields a marvelous and potent tool in the Force, and she should be ready to use it on behalf of a good cause.

((Updated Version: Although a Jedi toils to help others in need, he must sometimes suspend his wishes and let others impart assistance instead; even if the Jedi could perhaps do a better job (or act more quickly or easily). The Jedi should assist only as the situation requires, offer advice upon request, warn when necessary, and argue if proper reason fails. Otherwise, the Jedi must remember that his training is a potent tool and he should be ready to use it on behalf of a good cause.))

Reality - Jedi aren't the end all be all solution. You are not the answer to all problems everywhere. And by trying to be, by seeking to always be the leader, by always shouldering the responsibility of leadership you hinder those around you. Can you do it better? Maybe, but how is anyone going to learn to be as good or better or even just improve if they are not given the opportunity?

Say you are at a car accident. How can you best serve/help? Sometimes it is simply aiding law enforcement by placing your own road flairs. Letting the Emergency Responders know you have certification and are willing to help if needed. That may mean simply keeping others out of the way. It may mean following directions and being part of a search group. It is about giving your support and sometimes that support means standing back and shutting up.

As a Jedi you can lead by example. A calm, collected, and rational presence can provide much needed support in any heated situation. Just having that element can ease a situation and get it to move in a much more amicable direction. Support those in the leadership position, you don't need to always be the one in-charge. Likewise, when someone else is in-charge help them succeed. Team effort.

-= Lesson Four - Day Five Assignment =-

How about just a Q and A. You have any questions? Comments? Observations? Examples? Concerns? Issues? Thoughts? Opinions? Share.

Lesson Five - Day One:
Delusions of Grandeur

"The Jedi required generations to master the Force. Bit by bit, they discovered its secrets until they understood how to consistently attain the same results when using it, proving to themselves and the rest of the civilized galaxy that the Force was neither a hoax nor a fluke." - Power of the Jedi sourcebook.

Generations. Even the fictional inspiration which we draw upon acknowledges that mastery is not to be had right away. You may find claims to the counter in the larger Jedi Community online. People who say the they can perform fantastical feats (telekinesis for example). You will find those that say the legwork has already been done by other paths, citing sources like Qigong (Chi Kung). Yet the bare-knuckles reality is that the Force, defined however you wish, is not a proven scientific fact in any means resembling the fiction.

The point here is to remove thoughts of mastery, of psychic powers, of proving the validity of the Jedi Path by some mystical means. The Force is ineffable carrying a lot of definitions within our community. That is not a bad thing or even a hindrance. In fact it allows us to see more clearly the similarities, the areas and practices which our different beliefs overlap. This is the beauty of our diversity in the Jedi Path.

Listen (or read, as it were), the Jedi Path is about getting You in a proper place to better help others. How can you help others if you are a sinking ship? World-Betterment by means of Self-Betterment. The focus here isn't on the fictional, on the fantastical. No Astral Projection, No Psychic Powers, No Magical Cures.

What you will find here is an encouragement that you can indeed overcome anything in your life. You do so by Dedication, Self-Discipline, Patience, Hard Work, Knowledge. By taking responsibility and fighting through the pain of life to become something, someone, better. There is nothing you cannot do, this includes being a Jedi Knight. Like being a Jedi it may take years of work, commitment, and sacrifice, but in the end your goals, your dreams are something that you can place in your hands.

In the end I fully believe the Jedi Path offers something much better than lightsabers and force powers. Though lightsabers are cool and hard to beat. Still, I feel that what the Jedi Path imparts, the things one can take away from it greatly offer much more substantial gifts and abilities. And hopefully that concept has been enforced for the past month.

-= Lesson Five Assignment =-

Incorporating Jedi Practices into Your Life - Daily. Part Two
NOTE: <u>These are not to replace or be replaced by your current studies and activities.</u> Meaning, if you already do a specific meditation, you are still to practice what is listed here. If you work-out and cover these exercises you are still to do them at some point. <u>These are supplemental exercises for daily use</u>, to be used in conjunction with your current lifestyle.

- <u>Physical Fitness</u> - Start with some light stretching (touch the toes, reaching for the sky, etc.). A little knee high marching in place. Now - 20 Jumping Jacks, 10 Weighted Lunges (if no weights add 10 reps - so 25), 10 Weighted Push-up Raises (15 if no weights), 20 Weighted Squats (25 if no weights), 15 Hip Raises, 20 Mountain Climbers, 20 V-ups, and 15 Weighted Burpees. Daily, Once, any time; I recommend morning right when you get out of bed. Usually doesn't take me more than 10 minutes to complete, however on slow/tired days it can take 15 minutes. Pictures At the End. As a side-note, you can rest, mid-set break, but accomplish the numbers given. Seek to knock them out bam bam bam.

- <u>Meditation</u> - As written by Osho:
The whole secret of meditation is to be neither for or against, but unconcerned, cool, without any likes and

dislikes. Meditation is a simple method. Your mind is like a TV screen. Memories are passing, images are passing, thoughts, desires, a thousand and one things are passing; it is always rush hour.... One has to watch the mind without any evaluation, without any judgment, without any choice, simply watching unconcerned as if it has nothing to do with you and you are just a witness.... You can lose you witnessing in two ways either being for or against.... If you can manage even a few moments of that witnessing, you will be surprised how ecstatic you become.

At least once a Day you shall practice being a witness, a passive observer of your mind. The goal to be aware without judgment. Give at least 15 minutes of practice (in one sitting) daily. Record your thoughts and observations.

• <u>Awareness</u> - Find Life. Every single room you go into seek to find life. Note the obvious, seek the less obvious. People, plants, insects, find at least one living thing every single place you find yourself. Find the ant, find the cactus, be aware of all the life in any given room/place you find yourself. The people, the plants, all of it.

• <u>Diplomacy</u> - A key part of diplomacy is recognizing value. Value in tools, in others, in yourself, in knowledge. A true diplomat understands the value of all information in any given situation. This week acknowledge the information offered and find the information not given freely. Find the value in all involved parties/aspects. In every given situation what offers value? Is there anything not of value?

• <u>Self-Discipline</u> - Do I seriously even have to write anything here? Get to it Jedi.

Today's Assignment:

Personal Wellness is a core part of the Jedi Path. How would you rate your wellness? On a scale of 1 to 10. 1 being poor and 10 being excellent -- how do you feel your current level of

well-being is at?
Physical Well-Being:
Mental (intelligence) Well-Being:
Emotional Well-Being:
Social Well-Being:
Environmental Well-Being:
Financial Well-Being:
Due Today.

Exercise Pictures:
Jumping Jacks: Feet together, arms at your sides, jump spreading your feet shoulder width apart and bring your arms above your head all in one motion.

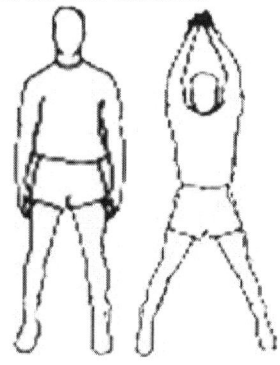

Weighted Lunges: Stand, comfortably, extend one leg forward, bending at the knee. Do Not let your other knee hit the ground. Stand back up, alternate legs.

Weighted Push-up Raises: Normal Push-up with the addition that when you reach the up position lift one arm up. Bringing the weight(hand) to your chest.

Weighted Squats: Normal Squat with the addition of raising your arms when you reaching the up position.

Hip Raise: Lay with your back flat on the ground with knees bent - as if doing sit-ups. Now simply raise your hips off the ground while keeping your shoulders on the ground. Creating a straight diagonal line from knees to shoulders.

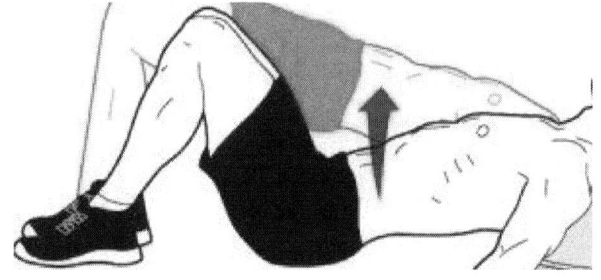

Mountain Climbers: Get into the starting Push-up Position. Now, you push off with your leg, bring the knee into the chest, while the other leg stays extended. Kick your leg back and bring the other knee into the chest.

V-ups: Lay on your back, flat on the ground. Arms extended above your head. Legs out straight. Bring your arms over and in front of you, reaching toward your toes. At the same time lift your legs up. And bringing your shoulders and back off the floor. Lay back down bringing your arms back over your head.

Weighted Burpee: Stand up straight. Squat down, kick your feet out so you are in the Push-up position. Do a Push-up. Bring your feet back in. Stand up. (If feeling froggy raise your hands/weights

to the sky)

Lesson Five - Day Two:
Lightsaber Syndrome

  Lightsaber Syndrome is my preferred fun way of talking about the dangers of Self-Empowerment. A very serious subject which all individuals must face who are bettering themselves. Before I get into the subject I want to talk a bit about where the title comes from. This does pertain to the lesson itself and what we are trying to convey and talk about.

  Lightsaber Syndrome comes from the 1998 role-playing game companion guide called Power of the Jedi. It is a source book to help those seeking to play Jedi characters understand their philosophy, their ideals, and psychology. Why Jedi do what they do and how it is taught to them. What the basis of being a Jedi is all about. What kind of person, what kind of character is a Jedi, and tips in how to be a Jedi in-game. Within this book is a small section which is labeled Lightsaber Syndrome and is a warning against the wrong mindset in being/playing a Jedi within the game. It is as follows:
Quote

Martial artists who reach a certain level of expertise might look forward to an opportunity to use what they have learned. They think: "I'm just waiting for somebody to give me grief, so I can wipe the floor with him." Sometimes they get tired of waiting and actually become more belligerent and aggressive, in hopes of provoking someone into starting a fight. They have forgotten - or never quite accepted - that martial arts are about self-defense, not showing off what they have learned.

Some role-players who choose Jedi characters fall into the same mentality. Carrying a lightsaber and having Force skills presents a tremendous temptation to use them, and some players get anxious waiting for an opportunity to do so in the game. As a result, they begin practicing some very un-Jedilike behavior - attacking first, trying to solve every problem with the Force, and deliberately creating situations that might allow them to roll their dice.

Usually, just pointing out that a player is suffering from "lightsaber syndrome" is enough to get him to take a step back and examine his actions. If not, the GM (Game Manager) may have to talk with the player out of game and clarify the role of the Jedi somewhat, especially how it pertains to her campaign. Remember, though, that there's nothing wrong with a player wanting to get involved in the game, unless it's disruptive. The player may just need a refresher on the Jedi Philosophy to get back into character.

    I find this a key reminder for all Jedi. It is a core foundation for anyone who empowers themselves. With actual Jedi philosophy we are talking about adding new tools into our toolbox. We are ensuring that we are capable and prepared to handle the plethora of challenges life throws our way. We do learn self-defense, we do learn the power of our words and how to use them, we do gain abilities which many in life simply do not worry about. Because of this one may be tempted to dig into that newly stocked toolbox and right some past wrongs. Or they may just be itching to put someone in their place.
    It is not uncommon, it is not something that we haven't seen before. Some come to the Jedi Path because they are seeking to be empowered. They are tired of being pushed around, of being bullied, of allowing others to determine the direction of their life. And it is an amazing thing to learn the power of No, the power of Me, of I, to find the strength within yourself to shoulder the responsibility of you and your actions. But there is a need for caution.
    An over-developed sense of justice can develop from such individuals. An aggressive streak can develop. An 'I'm going to bully the bully' mentality can set in. It is very freeing to tell someone off who has held power over you for so long. It can be a

very invigorating experience to finally understand that you had been giving the power away all along and you no longer have to just sit there and take it from people.

None of this is inherently bad or negative. However it can cloud one's mind, it can blind one to the consequences of their actions and the long term effects of their choices. It can also lead one away from the core aspects of the Jedi philosophy, of the applied ideals found within our path. Thus we offer this as a caution to your personal growth. Seek world-betterment via self-betterment, seek self-empowerment and empower others through it, yet ensure your actions represent the path you walk. Be an example to follow rather than a cautionary tale.

-= Lesson 5 - Day Two assignment =-

You are at the movies on a date. While waiting in line to buy tickets you notice five boys around 20 to 25 years of age. They are harassing another male of a similar age in a wheelchair who appears slightly mentally handicapped. The boys are calling name, pushing the chair, poking the person in the wheelchair; who has asked them to stop repeatedly.

Your date looks at you and says, "Do something." As a Jedi, how do you resolve the situation?
-=-
Give an example of resolving the situation with lightsaber syndrome.
-=-
What is the difference? Why should you try one way over the other?

Due ASAP.

Lesson Five - Day Three:
Exerting the Power of Self (a.k.a. Becoming the Bully)

In my life I have seen over and over the bullied become the bullies. When the down-trodden find strength and power within themselves they find the temptation to exert their new found abilities over others. It is why the weakest of people end up with a gun and hurting innocent people and look for the easy way out (suicide). It is outside power given to those with no inner power. Cowards who think themselves Martyrs.

The Jedi Path empowers the Self. Physical, Mental, Emotional, even Spiritual and Social Well-Being/Improvement. The first steps of the Jedi Path is self-betterment. Many who come to the Jedi Path have experienced the terror of being completely helpless, powerless, we have been in situations which have made us all too aware of our failings as humans. As such we sought a Path which spoke to the ability to not only help others, but help ourselves as well. It speaks to our desire to ensure others do not suffer as we had.

Yet because of that there is a passion, a zeal to defend, to protect, to use our abilities and new-found power to exert control over others. Our reasoning and intentions are good, but we are blinded and pushed by our desire to better the world, to ensure others do not suffer. In this the bullied becomes the bullies. We find power outside of ourselves because to truly conquer the self would mean putting out that fire, that passion against abuse in all forms. And then what are we? Just another delusional self-help group at best.

So where is the line? Where is the balance? What is the answer? What is the point?

Stability. True Strength. True Power. That is the Point and Purpose of the Jedi Path. The Tyrant is not Powerful. The Bully is not Powerful. Confidence, Belief in the Self, the Ability to overcome adversity without stepping on others, without throwing others under the bus, the ability to raise above with pushing others down. That is where true power is to be found; within the self. True power is dependent on one person and one person alone - You. And guess what? You are more than capable.

When you no longer have to prove someone else wrong in order to be right - that is when you have found power that no one else can touch. You can achieve much, protect many, lead as an example, if you only learn that your strength is not measured by those outside of yourself. People can try to restrict your choices, they can seek to exert control over you, but you always have the power of choice, the ability to make your own way, the power to determine your own fate. No one but you can determine the direction of your life. It is your life, it is in your hands, do not use any excuse or pass any blame. Be Who You Want To Be. It is for you to chose - no one else.

The Jedi Way is not found in exerting control and power over others. Being the Bully to Bullies is not the Jedi Way. When you are stable within yourself, when you have nothing to prove to no one, and yet you still reach for the stars? That is when you have found the Jedi Path. When you have the strength to be You regardless of the world around you - that is when you embody the Jedi Way.

-= Lesson 5 - Day 3 Assignment =-

A person has come to the JAO. They claim to be a Jedi Master recognized as such at several other Jedi sites. They cite black belt and reiki master certifications and accomplishments. Lets call them Berkilak. As Berkilak engages in conversations on our site, they start to use personal information to maliciously attack an individual on a personal level. Berkilak makes a case for why this person (they are attacking) is not a Jedi, is hurting the name, and has done bad things in the past. They state they are standing up against a fake Jedi who is dishonoring the Jedi Path. Despite being asked to stop and warned against their behavior Berkilak continues to personally attack anyone who engages them.

You are the JAO Administrator. You have complete power over the site. You also have personal knowledge of Berkilak. You have information of misconduct, of deceit, information which would completely humiliate them. What do you do? How do you resolve the situation?
-=-

Do you feel your solution falls under 'becoming the bully' tactics/mentality? Why or Why Not? As a Jedi how do you seek to ensure that you avoid becoming the bully?
Due ASAP.

Lesson Five - Day Four:
Fiction Can Be Fun....

One of the core aspects of the Jedi Path is aspiring to be like the fictional inspiration. To be that calm, objective, leader able to face the most extreme circumstances without sacrificing our ideals. Without sacrificing what makes you - you. We look to the fiction for that nudge in the direction we want to live. We look at quotes and determine if they are not only viable, but useful, beneficial, having a positive impact on our lives and those around us.

Peace, Calm, Relaxed. Having an unshakable center which allows us to face life head on and never feeling like we have to bury our head in the sand. Some of the fiction works to this advantage. It inspires us to be better, to be stronger, to be wiser, to see the bigger picture, and act with understanding and tolerance. And there are other quotes, other elements of the fiction which just don't add up in our daily lives. They are indeed meant merely for the entertainment of the story and saga.

Since 1996 people have been online seeking to live as Jedi in their everyday lives. Due to this there have been many who have contributed to the growth of the Jedi Path. In this we have grown beyond merely looking and analyzing Yoda quotes. And yes, in 1996, that was a major facet of Jedi training. These days, not so much, because we have over a decade of real-life experience to draw upon. We have trial-and-error of our senior Jedi. We have writings and texts which describe the aspects of the Jedi Path which have yield great results.

This doesn't, and in my opinion won't ever, dismiss or even replace the fictional inspiration. It is important to not only remember what inspired us, who inspired us, but it gives that end ideal. To one day in future generations be something like what inspired us. Not possible now and not possible in 100 hundred years are two every different things. One can look at history to see that - to see the ease in which advancements can be made and lost and rediscovered again.

The fiction is a part of who we are and what we do, but it is not the end-all-be-all. We do not look to memorize "*you will know. When calm, at peace, passive*" we seek to embody that. It doesn't matter if you can name the character and movie it comes from. What matters is living it, thus meditation, objectivity, emotional stability being a core part of the Jedi Path. Because Yoda said so? Because George Lucas wrote it? No, it is because fans lived it and found it to be a good and beneficial way to live.

Sure these fictional elements provided the entertaining transmission of ideals. Yet because it was beholden to no singular source, authors, writers, and all involved could draw upon multiple sources. This lead to a singular concept which isn't a mirror of any one preexisting path. Instead the Jedi have been and continue to evolve into a Path uniquely our own. Derived from fiction made into reality through the experiences of everyday people, like you and me.

-= Lesson 5 - Day 4 Assignment =-

Time to Play Real or Fictional. I am going to list five quotes. You are going to tell me if they are from a real Jedi source (someone like myself) or a fictional Jedi source (role-playing book, obi-wan, et cetera). Also I'd like you to offer why you think it is that. If just a feeling or a guess, that is fine, simply state as such. And while this should go without saying - no cheating, no throwing the quote into google or anything of that nature.

1.) "Peace is not the result of a strong emotional drive but rather a clear, dispassionate goal for the Jedi. Peace born of anger is no peace at all, and cannot last."
2.) "The Jedi Path is more than just thinking about Jedi ideals and meditating on the force, its about being a Jedi and living it."
3.) "Learn to recognize when speed is not important. Race when being first is important; move at your ow pace at all other times. It is not necessary to always strike the first blow, to provide the first solution, or to reach a goal before anyone else. In fact, it is

sometimes vital to strike the last blow, to give the final answer, or to arrive after everyone else."

4.) "A Jedi is at her best when she is brave, selfless, and responsible, and she puts the will of the Force before her own personal wants and needs. A Jedi also serves as an icon of socially acceptable behavior and positive influence."

5.) "Part of being a Jedi, for me, is about going beyond the place where I need to define who I am with colors, or words. It's about knowing who I am in such a way that I don't need to describe it - I just need to be it."

Due Today.

Lesson Five - Day Seven:
Your Path, Your Journey, Your Choice...

One thing often overlooked on the Jedi Path is the current medium of training. The majority of training takes place online, in-between life (meaning you train before or after work/school). Yet one applies being a Jedi into every facet of life. During school, work, family get-together, holidays, stress, fun, amusement parks, county fairs, jury duty, doctor appointments. This can be difficult in the beginning to really apply the Jedi Ideals to everything you do.

We have seen there are quite a few ideals to apply as well. And remembering them all can be a challenge in itself. Especially so early on in the training. The reality of living as a Jedi is one few suspect. It is my hope that we can change that in the future. To keep closer to our fictional inspiration while at the same time being very practical and applicable within today's society. However, as it stands right now the Jedi lifestyle is going to be a bit different than what one may hope for.

You have at the very least two years of training ahead of you. This training isn't as cool or hands-on as Luke Skywalker in Dagobah. This training is study, reading, and applying ideals, practices, and lessons to your life. It will be boring at times. Seem not worth it at others. "What does this lesson matter?" Is a question that will come up more than once during your time training. You will need to make changes in your thought process, how you live, how you act/react.

As such, you will change. No one is born a Jedi. We were free to live and act as we wished up to the point we chose to be Jedi. Being a Jedi means living a life of restrictions, of rules, and regulations. There are things you can do and things you cannot do. This is the life we live, one bound by the guidelines of our Path. The Jedi Circle, the Jedi Rules of Behavior, the Jedi Method, these all factor in from this point forward.

Guess what? People are not going to like this change. Well some might, but you will encounter times when people note and discourage the change. Most people just do not care about actual solutions, they just want to complain about a problem, not actually fix it. Thus to have someone practical, logical, with emotional stability looking at a situation? Not as fun as having someone sitting there complaining and getting emotional with them.

What you really want to do is look at the Jedi lifestyle. Is a life of emotional stability, logic, reason, objectivity, truly for you? Do you want to be the responsible one all the time? Knowing the responsibility will always fall to you? The more you train the more capable you become. The more capable you become, the more responsibility falls on your shoulders. Your excuses start falling to the wayside. Is that how you want to live your life? Helping others is a great goal, but that help is not always what people want. A Jedi gives what people need, not what they want.

A Jedi in today's society has no missions or temple. They have web sites and a long road of training, and preserving knowledge. Instead the Jedi of today have to worry about safeguarding the history and work of the Community they belong too. And honoring that inspiration and history by becoming examples of actual Jedi thought and practice. This is the mission of the Jedi today, to become actual Jedi Knights in thought, action, and speech. It is in this way that the Jedi will eventually grow into an actual order like we have come to see in the movies. And what will guide that action, thought and speech? Jedi Philosophy.

There are a lot of stipulations, a lot of changes. You have to adapt to situations and people at a moments notice. You have be constantly aware and focused. You will received a few thanks during that time, but mostly it is a thankless lifestyle. And at times instead of thanks you will get yelled at, insulted, and told off. All to wake-up and do it again tomorrow.

-= Lesson 5 - Day 5 Final =-

Self-Assessment:
Place yourself in the shoes of a Jedi Master. Read over your journal. Consider each overall lesson (lesson 1, rather than lesson 1, day 1). On a scale of 1 to 5, 5 being the best, how do you feel it rates? Then look at the overall Tier One Program up to this point. How would you assess your performance? Were you giving half-thought-out answers? Rushing? Vague? Would you, as a Jedi Master, consider the material good for someone just starting out on the Jedi Path? All this can be done in your own head. Meaning, you do not have to share if you do not wish. However, I do want your overall evaluation. Would you, as the Teacher, Pass or Fail yourself based upon your own performance? What were your strengths? What weaknesses do you feel are shown and can be worked upon?
Due in Two Days.

Supplemental Lessons

Supplemental Lesson 1: The Jedi Method.

I want to talk a bit about the Jedi Formula. Jedi Intent + Jedi Actions = Jedi Outcome. This is the most basic principle and formula for a Jedi to live by. It is very simplistic and works from a logical application of knowledge. We will be looking look at the formula itself and explain the how and the why of it working.

As Jedi we are often questioned as to why we do what we do. Especially by those involved and affected by our decisions and/or advice. They may feel or simply not understand how or why we act in the manner we do and look at situations in the manner we do. They may feel we must be lying, or wrong about something somewhere, that we must be allowing our selfish wants and emotions to dictate our actions and thoughts. However the formula for Jedi (re)action is very simple. Jedi Intent + Jedi Action = Jedi Outcome. This is how we, as Jedi, ensure that our outcomes have the best possible outcome we can give at the time. Even if that means recognizing that it would be better to let someone else handle the situation.

Now every Jedi is aware of the basics of Jedi ideology. This can be seen in the Jedi Code, Jedi Rules of Behavior, and the Jedi Circle. Which this book offers for one to apply to their life. And it is these texts that help one not only understand the Jedi Methods when dealing with any situation. But also help one define Jedi Intent, through purpose and definition. If one wishes to be a Jedi within today's society, it is this formula that will ultimately pave that road.

Jedi Intent is the first item in our equation and thus the first we must define and clarify. Jedi Intent is defined by the virtues of the Jedi Path; most simply put the desire to help others and make the world (even if our own little world) a better place. Which can be also be associated with the Five Goals of the Jedi. Briefly the five goals of the Jedi are as follows:

- <u>Train Diligently</u>: Be capable of fulfilling the role and course of a Jedi.
- <u>Provide Support</u>: Sometimes the best help, is merely encouragement and support. A Jedi does not always have to be hands-on, but instead provides the needed support.
- <u>Render Aid</u>: Sometimes it is resources that are needed the most. A Jedi can give their time, money, services, and/or supplies for the service of others.
- <u>Defend Those in Need</u>: Sometimes people need help defending themselves. Whether that is by sticking up for them in an argument or unfair situation. Calling the proper authorities to correct a situation. Or showing that they have someone who will not allow physical harm to come to them. A Jedi defends those in need.
- <u>Study of the Force</u>: A Jedi continues the study and advancement of the Force. Further defining the Force, by continually experiencing, exploring, and understanding.

So we can look at Jedi Intent and associate it with the selfless desire to change the world for the better. And if we wanted to make it is as simplistic as possible we could merely say that Jedi Intent equals the intent to help people for the better (long term and short term).

Next we come to what seems the most misunderstood of the formula. When in all actuality this is the most simplistic and easy to understand. Jedi Action is just expressing Jedi Ideology. Jedi actions (and reactions) includes restrictions on how one acts (emotionally stable, calm, at peace, etc.). As well as directs specific action; diplomacy, awareness, patience, self-discipline, meditation, objectivity, reliability, and so on and so forth. Again a clear definition of this can be seen within the Jedi Circle (listed on page).

Jedi action is clearly defined within the Philosophy of the Jedi, even within the Jedi Code. Obviously it is not a singular line of thought and it certainly does not limit the Jedi to one singular action. You give five different Jedi the same scenario you'll most likely get five different solutions. Likewise, it does not allow for just anything, it does not say do whatever works. There is a guideline, a method of how to go about acting and reacting in any given situation.

There is very clear ideology associated with the Jedi. Very specific ideals which govern a Jedi's actions and process. These are not subjective, but very clearly listed and have proven correct over years of experience and trial and error. So very clearly we can see that Jedi Action equals Jedi Code, Jedi Circle, Jedi Rules of Behavior. I will not include those within this section, but one can find each of these explained in-depth throughout this book.

Lastly we come to the end of the situation. We want a desired outcome obviously. We are seeking a Jedi Outcome, meaning we want an outcome that helps the greatest number of people involved with the greatest good in mind, especially in the long term. From the previous statements we can see Jedi seek to be peaceful, helpful, and beneficial for all parties involved. We seek to do this without compromising ourselves, our ideals, or belittling those people we are seeking to help. This is important as we want all our hard work to help not harm. But the trick is understanding the difference between a temporary outcome and a long-term outcome. Sometimes the Jedi Outcome results in harsh feelings and words thrown back at the Jedi, however a couple months down the road one can see the benefits of the Jedi Action; thus understanding the Jedi Intent and finally gaining the full effect of the Jedi Outcome. It may not be what we wanted or expected, but more often than not, it is what is needed. A direct result of Jedi Intent combined with Jedi Action.

The Jedi Outcome is simply the most beneficial outcome for all parties involved. With the ideology of the saying; "Give a man a fish, feed him for a day. Teach a man to fish, feed him for a lifetime." - Chinese Proverb We are looking to help people to help themselves. We want the common good to benefit and have a lasting effect.

Hopefully one can very clearly see how this very simple

process works. In other terms one would simply say: Live as a Jedi, see Jedi results. Breaking that down we see the formula, Jedi Intent + Jedi Action = Jedi Outcome. It is just living as a Jedi everyday of your life. In every single thing you do, living, acting, and reacting like a Jedi. We see that in order to arrive at the proper outcome, one must intend to be a Jedi and thus follow through by acting like a Jedi. And in the end they will be a Jedi, which directly affects the outcome of any situation.

In conclusion, we look at the question of what defines a Jedi. How they act and react. They are defined by what they do. Really there is only so many ways to state that a Jedi lives and acts as a Jedi (as directly defined by the Jedi Circle) and that defines them. Jedi Intent + Jedi Action = Jedi Outcome. One can seek to argue the importance of one over the other, but you'll just be going in circles. Quite obviously they require each other.

One cannot be a Jedi if they do not intend to be a Jedi. If they do not have the intentions of a Jedi. One cannot be a Jedi by just doing whatever they want. They must act as a Jedi. In order to arrive at the most Jedi-like outcome you need to intend to approach it like a Jedi and you need to act/react as a Jedi.

Nothing is perfect and there are going to be times when things do not go according to plan or how we had hoped. But to help ensure the best outcome we can as Jedi, we hold to what makes us Jedi. And accept the consequences (whether positive or negative) of our involvement. And all anyone can ask of a Jedi is to be a Jedi. It is all we, as a group, can ask of you - if you choose to carry the Jedi name. You will face challenges, you will not always succeed, but this is a Path of continual growth and learning. So simply do your best to adhere to this simple method while living as a Jedi.

Old FA Lesson:
Light Jedi: Lecture #6
Freedom through restraint

A Jedi has a particular ally on his or her side...moral value. Some may feel that this has a definite restriction on the different aspects of the Force that a Light Side Jedi may use, and they are correct in their beliefs...to an extent. A Light Side Jedi is restricted in that he or she must always do the morally just thing in a given situation. It is our belief that in every situation, there is a solution with a positive outcome. As Light Side Jedi, that is a strong example of our optimistic point of view. What of situations where there is no truly positive outcome, where the loose ends do not tie up perfectly? It is at this point that a Jedi has two responsibilities. The first responsibility entails finding a strong solution to the problem, using Light Side means. The second responsibility is a "Plan B" sort of action...utilize the most morally just of your options, to obtain the best solution possible. Sometimes, this may not be an incredibly positive solution. But rest well in the knowledge that you have attempted to do your best. This brings up the point of "Do, or do not. There is no try." This does not lock in an absolutely positive solution. This simply means that you are to DO the best you can, not TRY to do the best you can. This means that you are to DO what is right, not TRY to do what is right. And, last but not least, you are to DO what you have set out to accomplish. You are not to TRY for a lesser solution. Once you have set your eyes on a path that you have judged to be the most humane, the most positive, you are to follow that path, wherever it may lead you. Again and again, the point is stressed that we are to use Light Side techniques in the belief that no matter how they are used, any use of Dark Side techniques leads to a Dark end result.

A Jedi finds peace in helping others. We are without conflict within ourselves because we believe in our cause. We have no decisions to make regarding which is the right path to choose...the right path is the path that is right. It is through our idealism, through helping others, that we find out roots in the force, and find something to believe in. We exist to improve upon things...and to bring light to an otherwise dark world.
JediKnightG

:: **Assignment** ::

Scenario: You on a lifeboat from a cruise ship. Due to circumstances, there is only you, a pregnant woman, and an elderly man. Your life boat was damaged a is slowly taking on water. If one person was removed from the boat, the leak would slow enough to make it to safety. If no one is removed everyone dies. Who do you remove from Lifeboat? Why? How does this fit with Jedi Intent? How does this fit with Jedi Action? Is the Outcome of Intent and Actions a Jedi Outcome? Explain.

Supplemental Lesson Two: The Force.

There is no quick answer or lesson to be had with the Force. Some see the Force and think cool oobie powers, like telekinesis, moving things with the mind. They think Jedi Mind Trick, how cool would that be? But even if these tricks are possible, that is not an answer to the Force. And offers little understanding of the Force. If you want to learn about the Force, you first have to forget such ideas as Force Powers. That should not be a goal for a Jedi. A Jedi is a Jedi because of how they live, not because they have unlocked some mystical trick.

The truth about the Force is that we do not have a definite answer for it. It can be classified in many ways. And while most go with a more paranormal or supernatural view, I like to think of the Force as an idea. An idea to live up to, an idea to follow. It is said that the Force is created by all living things. It connects us and binds the galaxy together. What a wonderful idea to guide someone. An idea that what we do effects us all.

It is not a new idea or one which is solely the Jedi's. However it is a great guide to action. We are connected, there is a flow between us all and our actions, our reactions, effect all we are connected to and change the flow that surrounds us. You can break this down into two different well-known principles. The first being, treat others how you would like to be treated. And the second being a cause and effect principle, an understanding that your choices do have effects and consequences, thus one should not act/react carelessly.

We can say that the Force is an energy field. And we would have basic science to support us to a point. We could say the Force is the mysteries that reside in our brains, human will, our drive to not only survive, but to excel. We could compare the Force with other established ideas such as Tao in Taoism. Or the Holy Spirit in Christianity. Or we could compare it to ideas of Chi/Ki as present via Qigong. In the end, the source material doesn't really matter to the Jedi Path, because it is an ideal.

Sure, if you want oobie powers and fancy party tricks, you need to have a clear understanding of the source. If you are seeking immortality then you would need to have pure understanding of the essence of life. If you are seeking to move objects with a wave of your hand, than you need to understand the principles to make that happen. But if that is your goal, then you are better suited looking elsewhere. Plenty of paths out there that promise great rewards.

For me, I see the Force in known science, in the basic laws of physics. I see the Force in everyday life, in life in general. I see it in our five senses. Nothing really mystical, just the amazing way the universe seems to work and follow. I just have a different view than most. There are plenty focuses and ways to explore the Force. And that is something for each Jedi to chose for themselves.

That is what this boils down to in the end. We will explore the Force more in-depth in further tiers of this Academy. But that does not change nor should it change how one approaches the spiritual, the mystical. The answers of the Force are found within.

:: Assignment ::

Discovering the Force

What do think the Force is? Write in your journal your current view, as soon as you are done here. Does not have to be in-depth. After that take a week. Just take time to observe life. Stand for a few minutes in the backyard or park or forest, and just observe the trees, flowers, insects, life. Take time to sit outside a coffee shop and just people watch, observe as life moves on. Go for a walk and notice the ants, the spiders, the birds, the flora. Seek, during the week, to incorporate a time of reflection and observation. Feel free to add in some meditation if you so desire. Also consider looking into other ideas out there such as Tao, Chi, etc. At the end of the week re-approach the question - what is the Force?

Supplemental Lesson Three: The Dark Side.

Yoda: [points to a cave opening beneath a large tree] That place... is strong with the dark side of the Force. A domain of evil it is. In you must go.
Luke: What's in there?
Yoda: *Only what you take with you.*

The Dark Side a heavy topic within the Star Wars fiction. Which did not vary much in the early days of the Jedi Community. It was a scary subject, taboo for young students to even consider exploring. We have been given ideas on what the Dark Side is and how one falls to the Dark Side. Fear leads to Anger, et cetera. But is this reality or fiction? As one might guess, we will be exploring the Dark Side here.

The Dark Side that we are talking about however is not a Path or Label. The Cave is The Self. It is an Aspect of the Self. It is the lack of illumination. In otherwords it is the lack of understanding and knowledge. Much like the fiction we can say that the Dark Side blinds us, it dominates our existence, it has a chain effect (one leading to the next). Yet we all have the Darkness within us. There are truths we refuse to face, there are elements of the self we do not confront, there a demons and skeletons left unchecked.

This is the true danger of the Dark Side, our lack of confronting it. We as Jedi feel a plethora of emotions. Some have labeled these emotions positive and negative, but that is a misunderstanding. We feel good when happy, thus we label it positive. And feel bad when sad, thus negative. Yet truly emotions are simply indicators. Just as ignorance on a subject is not negative, it simply indicates we have something new to learn, an opportunity for growth.

Thus to over come the Dark Side we need only confront it. And we tend to find the truth in the allegory of the Cave, *only what you take with you.* Thus we seek to shed the light of understanding upon it. Why did I react that way? Why am I acting this way? Why do I feel this way? facing the unpleasant truths along with the beautiful truths. Coming to terms with the self, who we are and what we do. We if find something we might want to change about ourselves, we first have to acknowledge and accept that before we can move forward. We must face our caged demons within and come to understand them, their origins, and what we can do to either make peace with them or remove them.

Once we face the darkness within, the Dark Side loses its power over us. And we are able to move forward assured in our Path. Though do not become complacent. Seek to keep that open understanding of the self, re-evaluate from time to time, the Dark Side is never gone completely and we must keep a watchful eye to keep the light of understanding lit.

Luke: I won't fail you. *I'm not afraid.*
Yoda: You will be. *You... will... be.*

:: Assignment::
Facing the Darkness

Step 1 - Take five to ten minutes and look at yourself in the mirror. I want you to just take some time and really look at yourself. Try to get a body mirror or at least most of you in view. Take the time to just look at you, your body, your face, your eyes, get close, really look at yourself. Feel free to add some extra time and flex, make faces, dances a little, just as long as you keep the attention on you. Your shape, your movement, your height. Certain thoughts will no doubt pop up, things you like, things you don't like, perhaps things you hadn't really noticed before (which could be good or bad in your opinion). Take the time to be honest with yourself. And really be honest, you may not really like your eye color, but does that mean no one else could? Are they still nice eyes, just not the eyes you want? And please feel free to go over the time limit. This is just about you and getting to really know yourself. What do you like? What don't you like? In the end remember that there are things you can change, things you can't, and things you shouldn't. And we will get to that, but for now, just examine you deeply. And tell me - What did you discover?

Step 2 – ((This should be familiar – unless you skipped ahead. I am leaving this in here, because it was a part of the original lesson plan. And if some time has passed, it might be fun to do it again and compare.))

Time to face inward, examine and write out You. Please take a moment to relax, to center yourself, and be ready to reflect on the self. For this exercise I want you to fill in where I leave off. But I want to stress, two things. One, be completely honest. Two, you are just starting out (presumably) as a Jedi, don't feel you have to have an answer, or even a "*Jedi answer*". Just be honest. We will look at this later on down the line and see what changes may have taken place during your time and training as a Jedi here. This is for you, not to impress anyone.

I am
I share
I express
I build
I change
I comfort
I seek
I accumulate
I feel
I accept
I expand
We are

Step 3 - Take the week to reflect on your life thus far. Take some time to just reflect on the choices and things in your life, where you are at, where you want to be, etc. Reflect on failures, triumphs, miracles, lucky breaks, unlucky breaks.

Through out the week while reflecting on these things write them down (probably best in an offline journal). Perhaps tackle one a day. Monday reflecting on all the mistakes and bad decisions and what you learned from them. Tuesday reflecting on all the events that just seemed to come out of nowhere, those unlucky breaks, those miracles. And when writing them down, see if you can track down any cause and effect to them. See if you can track how some of them came into effect. Wednesday challenges you have overcame, triumphs in your life, successes. What did you learn from those events. And so on for the entire week.

Now again this should be more private and you can simply keep it offline and use it to really understand and get to know yourself. Take the week to really work on you, your dreams, your situation, your finances, et cetera.

Supplemental Lesson Four: The Jedi Religion.

Jediism - the Jedi as a Religion. In 2001 there was media attention to the Jedi Path. This was due to the United Kingdom Census and people listing Jedi as their Religion. A website called Jediism Way, added to the fever of a Jedi Religion by rallying behind the movement. People enlisted in the Military have listed Jedi as their religion to have it placed on their dog tags. In New Zealand a group of people has been known to hold 'service' for those of the Jedi Religion. All this adds to the confusion of the question; Is Jedi a religion? Is there such a thing as Jediism?

Before we get into this further it really is as simple as this. Jedi is a way you live. It is personal. It makes no demands on your religious beliefs. This means you can be a Jedi and Christian. Likewise you can indeed say Jedi is **your** religion. However as a group the Jedi is not a religion. Religious belief is respected and the Jedi encourage you to find your own answer.

Now all that said, here at the Jedi Academy Onine the view is that the Jedi Path is a lifestyle, it is a philosophy. It is a way we chose to conduct our lives within the world. There is no form of worship, no set doctrine, prayers or ceremonies. Could there be? Yes, it wouldn't be difficult to create all bells and whistles which most religions tote. In fact many groups which cling to the title Jediism have gone out of their way to provide these elements. But the Jedi as a whole are not a religious organization, we are a philosophy, a belief in action. A diverse group of individuals who have come to train, learn, share and grow together. We share our different faiths and religions, even those that follow Jediism.

Out of the several Jedi in our community, our beliefs differ in terms of worship and religion. We have Jedi who are Christian, Wiccan, Catholic, Buddhist, Jewish, Muslim, Agnostic, and those who have a belief that doesn't fit into any organized religion.

From this Jedi learn of different beliefs and cultures. While living as a Jedi you will come across many who have different beliefs and cultures, the first step in experiencing that is here with each other.

The Jedi Path is a Philosophical undertaking of living as a Jedi Knight. What we see in Star Wars is our biggest inspiration. And what we see are individuals who dedicated themselves to something that was within their ability to harness. It is this that separates us the most, the Jedi Path has no Deities, no prophets. Just good old fashion Human Ability.

In Star Wars the Force was not called or considered a God or a deity of any kind. Some would like to quote Han Solo "*hokey religions and ancient weapons*" and others quote Grand Moff Tarkin "*You, my friend, are all that's left of their religion.*" These weren't meant to state Jedi was a religion, but to show the common misunderstanding of an outsider. These characters were not Jedi and had limited understanding of the Jedi. No Jedi has stated that the Jedi Path is a religion within the fiction.

We are not looking to be a religion, we do not need to be one. We are not Scientology, we do not have worship or prayers or religious figureheads. Following a philosophical path is indeed a way of life, a core belief, but it is not a religion. We have our practices, we do not condemn others for their varied beliefs, we are simply not a religion. We are merely another path to walk in life.

This philosophy is something that speaks to certain people. It inspires them to grow and better themselves. They take it seriously, they train, study, practice, exercise, and overall grow as a person within the philosophy. It is a way of life they have chosen. A way of life which does not dictate their belief system. If an individual chooses to see the life energy of the world as God's creation than they are free to do that. If one wants to see the Force as the energy and impulses of the human brain and nervous system, they are free to do that.

No belief in a higher power is required here, just a desire to grow as a better person and the willingness to work hard for it.

While some may find similarities between this philosophy and other religions, that is truly no surprise. Most religions have something in common with each other and they certainly all have something in common with the various philosophical schools of thought out there, altruism being an example.

Case and Point: We have no theories on the Creation of the Universe and/or Man, We have no Ritual Observance of Faith (no worship, no prayers, no holidays), we do not say what happens when you die (no after-life speculation); it could even be said we have no spiritual thought as energy can be seen as science, not spiritual idealism. After-all if we considered energy worth worship we would have to start praying to the Energizer Bunny. People may try to twist definitions to claim the Jedi Path as a religion, they may try to package it as some sort of universalism ideal of religion, may claim religious freedom to see it as a religion, but in the end they only degrade the Jedi Path as a whole. At least that is what they have presented over the years in my experience.

What we must do now is see what your own studies uncover. Time to discover the answer for yourself. One last thing before we end here. As it is not know or clear. If one chooses to follow Jediism or say the Jedi is their religion, that is their choice. As mentioned, we do not tell any Jedi what to believe in terms of religion, from Atheism to Zionism - this includes one freedom to chose Jediism. However that is a personal choice and not on reflective of an entire Path or Organization.

:: Assignment ::

Research the Jedi Religion, find examples of it, from youtube videos to various websites. Compare these with the basic foundations of the Jedi Path (Code, Circle, Behavior). Also research the word Religion - The word itself has various definitions and uses (context in which it can be used). Now come to your own conclusions as to whether or not the Jedi Path is a religion. Is the Jedi Path a Religion? Share your conclusions, <u>in detail</u>, in your journal.

Conclusion

We have reached the end of our tier one program. Hopefully this has shed some light on living as a Jedi. Why we label it a philosophy. How Jedi live their lives daily and what we aspire to be. If this has been beneficial to you then you are more than welcome to join us at our website. We do have other books out there if you'd like to go that route. The Jedi Circle book is actually the old tier two program we use to run. We have long since upgraded, but it still provides more lectures, lessons, and assignments.

For me it has not been that long in writing this book. A lot of this stuff is just ingrained in my head. Another reason is some of this stuff I already have written out more than once for the website. So there is a easy transition and rewrite. Of course, I am a horrible writer so a lot of technical and artful elements of writing a book are completely missed by me. The point being is that I am not sure how long it has taken you to get here.

I like to imagine you have completed the first stages of a journey. That you have had some interesting experiences. Things which have taught you new things, affirmed older ideas, and simply allowed you to embrace all of life more. I like to think you just went through a growing period and you now find yourselves letting out the sigh of completion. The heavy breath of a job well done.

If you'd like to share your experience you should know where to find me. Online at the website I go by the name Opie Macleod. Opie is a nickname I had long before I found the Jedi. And when I did find the online Jedi community, well you just did not share your real name online. There was no facebook back then. You kept all your personal details very private. So I encourage you to drop me a line and tell me your experience with the book.

Take care and best wishes in your journey – wherever it may take you.

Resources

Website Links:
Jedi Academy Online – http://jediacademyonline.com
Real Jedi Knights (archived) - http://archive.jedifoundation.com/realjediknights/www.geocities.com/mi_zhe_fu/index.html

Extra Information:
Code of Conduct:
1.) No Spamming. Zero Tolerance - you spam you get banned.

2.) No Double-Accounts. There is simply no need what-so-ever to have two or more accounts on this board (unless you are an admin with a testing account). Again Zero-Tolerance.

3.) This place is a serious discussion forum. You are expected to act in a respectful and academic demeanor. There is a time and place (Alora Phoenix Forum mostly) to be silly and have fun. At all other times you should seek make the proper impression by being courteous.

4.) The above means no profanity. There is simply no reason to type out curse words. You are given time online, you can walk away from the computer, take a break before replying, in this there is no reason to react with insults and profanity. This is a family atmosphere, keep that way or you will be removed.

5.) Visitors and even some Members will not obey the above rules - this does not give you justification to respond in the same manner. You are responsible for your actions and reactions, just because a person is rude does not mean you are allowed to be just as rude.

6.) Do not make assumptions about people. Online interactions are hard to read. A lot can be missed in translating from verbal to written and vice versa. Just because you read something as insulting or hostile doesn't mean it was meant that way. Seek clarification, ask if unsure, express your view without accusing anyone. Misunderstanding do happen online, account for them, avoid them by being as clear as possible and seeking clarification when necessary.

7.) Please post in the proper forums.

8.) Please respect the levels used here. They are not easily accomplished and should be treated with an increasing level of respect. A Jedi of the Third Level is a hard-earned title that few are able to reach. So show the proper courtesy to those that have dedicated themselves and have achieved honorable positions within their path.

9.) This is a organization and path of many beliefs when it comes to religion. Respect people's choices in such beliefs. You may seek to discuss one's beliefs, if they are willing and only for educational purposes. Do not preach about your religion, do not seek to convert others, do not seek to change the beliefs of others. There is zero tolerance for any attacks on anyone's beliefs or lack thereof. God, Buddha, Spaghetti Monster, doesn't manner, religious beliefs are personal and are to be respected.

10.) We work with a three-strike policy for most transgressions (except the ones noted as zero tolerance). You will be given opportunities to show you have learned from your mistakes, however that patience is not infinite. Continued transgressions will mean you will be removed from this organization permanently. Fore-warned is fore-armed, most individuals here are Jedi and will be expected to act as such. If one is unable to act in a respectful demeanor they will deal with the consequences of their actions.

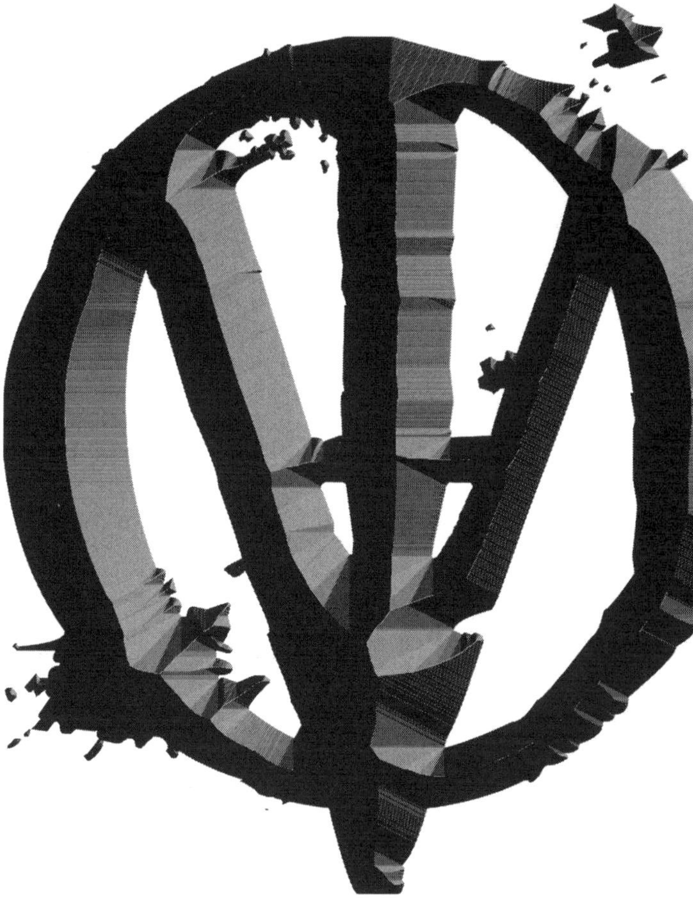

Printed in Great Britain
by Amazon